GREEN THREADS WARDROBE

EMBRACING ETHICAL AND SUSTAINABLE FASHION

DR. MINAKSHI BANSAL

DEDICATION

This book is dedicated to all the garment workers around the world, whose tireless efforts and creativity bring our clothes to life. May their voices be heard, their rights be respected, and their livelihoods be sustained.

♡♡♡

Contents

Contents

Contents

Prayer

"Om Bhadram Karnebhih Shrinuyama Devah

Bhadram Pashyemakshabhiryajatrah

Sthirairangais Tushtuvamsastanubhih

Vyashema Devahitam Yadayuh

Svasti Na Indro Vriddhashravah

Svasti Nah Pusha Vishwavedah

Svasti Nastarkshyo Arishtanemih

Svasti No Brihaspatir Dadhatu

Om Shantih Shantih Shantih"

This mantra is a prayer for universal well-being, invoking the blessings of various deities for protection, health, and happiness. It emphasizes the importance of experiencing the auspicious through all senses and living a life aligned with divine purpose. The repetition of "Shantih" at the end signifies a deep desire for peace in the individual, the environment, and the universe at large. This mantra is often recited as a prayer for peace, prosperity, and the physical and spiritual well-being of all beings.

🍃🍃🍃

About The Author

This book represents the culmination of extensive research and meticulous analysis, incorporating a diverse range of sources, including numerous books, scholarly studies, and personal experiences. Additionally, I have scoured various websites to gather relevant information and data essential for the compilation of this work. I have taken every precaution to ensure the accuracy of the information presented and have diligently cited all sources to acknowledge their contributions.

From her earliest days, Minakshi was distinguished by an insatiable appetite for reading. Her literary universe was inhabited by characters and narratives that spanned ethical tales, motivational and inspirational stories, and the mythic parables imbued with life lessons. This voracious reading habit was not merely for personal edification but was driven by a desire to distill and disseminate the essence of these narratives to foster the development of students and peers alike. She was particularly captivated by the lives and teachings of historical figures and spiritual leaders such as Adi Shankaracharya, Swami Vivekananda, Dr. APJ Abdul Kalam, Mahamana Pandit Madan Mohan Malviya, Mahatma Gandhi, Sardar Vallabhai Patel, and Vinoba Bhave, among others. Their philosophies and life stories fueled her ambition to embody their ideals of resilience, selflessness, and relentless pursuit of knowledge.

Dr. Minakshi's academic and practical engagement with psychology has been equally noteworthy. As a research scholar, her focus has been on exploring the intricate tapestry of the human psyche, aiming to unlock the potential for psychological well-being and societal harmony. Her scholarly work is complemented by her active involvement in social work, where she employs her academic insights to make tangible differences in the lives of the underprivileged. Her endeavours in social work are characterized by an innovative approach that combines traditional wisdom with contemporary psychological practices to address the multifaceted challenges faced by these communities.

Her artistic talents, another facet of her diverse capabilities, are not merely a personal passion but also serve as a medium through which she communicates and connects with others. Her art, rich in symbolism and emotional depth, reflects her philosophical inquiries and social concerns, offering viewers a glimpse into the breadth of her intellect and the depth of her compassion.

In addition to her contributions to the arts and social sciences, Dr. Minakshi has embraced the healing arts of Pranic Healing, mastering the techniques developed by Master Choa Kok Sui. This practice, which focuses on the manipulation of Prana or life energy to heal the body and aura, has been both a personal journey of discovery and a means through which she extends her healing touch to others. Her proficiency in Pranic Healing is complemented by her advocacy and teaching of various forms of meditation aimed at rejuvenation, personal betterment, and the cultivation of harmony within individuals and communities alike.

Dr. Minakshi's life is a narrative of relentless pursuit, not just of personal achievement but of the upliftment and empowerment of society at large. Her diverse interests and talents—spanning the arts, literature, psychology, and the healing practices—converge on a singular path of service. She embodies the spirit of the luminaries who inspired her, channelling their legacy through her actions and teachings. Through her books, art, and social initiatives, she continues to inspire a new generation to embark on their own journeys of self-discovery, resilience, and altruism.

Her commitment to social betterment, particularly her focus on uplifting underprivileged children, reflects a deep understanding of the transformative potential of education and personal development. By integrating her knowledge of psychology, her artistic sensibilities, and her healing practices, Dr. Bansal has developed a holistic approach to social work that addresses both the immediate needs and the long-term well-being of the communities she serves.

As an author, Dr. Minakshi's writings offer a blend of inspirational insights, practical wisdom, and reflective contemplations drawn from her extensive reading and life experiences. Her books serve as a guide for those seeking to navigate the complexities of life with grace, resilience, and purpose. Through her narratives, she extends an invitation to her readers to explore the depths of their own potential and to contribute meaningfully to the collective well-being of society.

In Dr. Minakshi Bansal, we find a remarkable synthesis of the artist, the scholar, the healer, and the social activist. Her life's work stands as a beacon of hope and a source of inspiration for individuals seeking to make a difference in the world. Her story is a compelling reminder of the power of individual action, rooted in compassion and driven by a profound commitment to the betterment of humanity. Dr. Minakshi's legacy is not just in the tangible outcomes of her efforts but in the enduring spirit of inquiry, empathy, and service that she embodies.

❦❦❦

Preface

As I embarked on the journey of writing this book, "Green Threads Wardrobe: Embracing Ethical and Sustainable Fashion," I was driven by a deep passion for fashion and a growing concern for its impact on our planet and society. Like many others, I have always been fascinated by the transformative power of clothing, the way it can express our individuality, boost our confidence, and even spark social movements.

However, I also became increasingly aware of the dark side of the fashion industry, the environmental degradation, the exploitation of workers, and the relentless cycle of consumerism that fuels it.

This realization led me on a quest to explore the world of sustainable fashion, to discover brands and designers who are committed to ethical practices, and to find ways to make more conscious choices about my own wardrobe. This book is a culmination of that journey, a guide for anyone who wants to embrace a more sustainable and ethical approach to fashion.

The fashion industry is at a crossroads. The traditional model of fast fashion, with its emphasis on cheap, trendy clothes and rapid production cycles, is no longer sustainable. It is wreaking havoc on our environment, contributing to pollution, waste, and resource depletion.

It is also exploiting workers, particularly in developing countries, who are often paid poverty wages and forced to work in dangerous conditions.

The good news is that there is a growing movement towards sustainable fashion. More and more brands and designers are recognizing the need to change their practices and are adopting more ethical and eco-friendly approaches. Consumers are also becoming more aware of the impact of their clothing choices and are demanding more sustainable options.

This book aims to empower readers to become part of this movement. It provides a comprehensive overview of the various facets of sustainable fashion, from the environmental and social impacts of fast fashion to the principles of ethical production, sustainable materials, and conscious consumption. It also offers practical tips and resources for building a sustainable wardrobe, discovering ethical brands, and making informed choices about our clothing purchases.

I believe that fashion can be a force for good in the world. It can empower individuals, celebrate diversity, and inspire creativity. But it can also be a tool for change, a way to challenge the status quo and advocate for a more sustainable and equitable future. By embracing sustainable fashion, we can not only reduce our environmental impact but also support ethical practices and contribute to a more just and compassionate world.

This book is not just for fashionistas or environmentalists; it's for anyone who cares about the future of our planet and the well-being of its people. It's for those who want to make a difference with their choices and use their voices to advocate for change. It's for those who believe that fashion can be both beautiful and ethical, stylish and sustainable.

As you embark on your own journey towards sustainable fashion, remember that every choice you make matters. Whether it's choosing a fair trade t-shirt over a fast fashion one, supporting a local designer, or simply mending a hole in your favorite sweater, your actions can have a ripple effect, inspiring others and contributing to a more sustainable future.

I hope that this book will inspire you to embrace sustainable fashion, to explore the many possibilities it offers, and to use your voice and your style to make a positive impact on the world. Remember, fashion is not just about what we wear; it's about who we are and what we stand for. By choosing sustainable fashion, we are choosing a future that is not only stylish but also ethical, responsible, and compassionate.

Dr. Minakshi Bansal
Social Activist
Ahmedabad, Gujarat, Bharat

ϼϼϼ

ONE

The Hidden Cost of Fast Fashion: Unveiling the Environmental and Social Impact

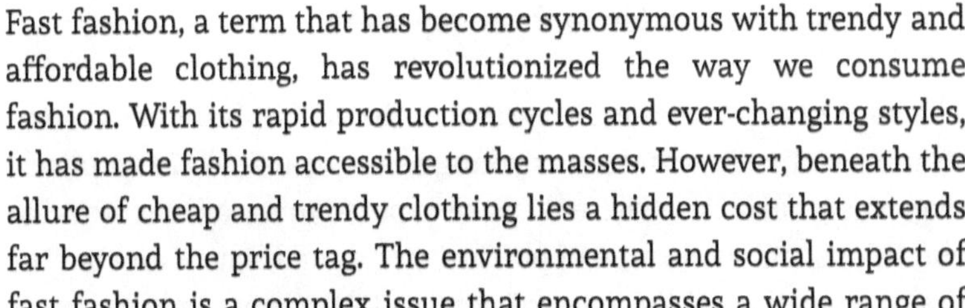

Fast fashion, a term that has become synonymous with trendy and affordable clothing, has revolutionized the way we consume fashion. With its rapid production cycles and ever-changing styles, it has made fashion accessible to the masses. However, beneath the allure of cheap and trendy clothing lies a hidden cost that extends far beyond the price tag. The environmental and social impact of fast fashion is a complex issue that encompasses a wide range of concerns, from resource depletion and pollution to labor exploitation and waste.

The environmental impact of fast fashion is staggering. The industry is a major contributor to greenhouse gas emissions, water pollution, and waste generation. The production of textiles requires vast amounts of water and energy, and the use of harmful chemicals in the dyeing and finishing processes can contaminate waterways and harm ecosystems. Additionally, the transportation of clothing from factories to stores and consumers around the world further adds to the industry's carbon footprint.

One of the most significant environmental concerns associated with fast fashion is the issue of textile waste. The industry's emphasis on disposable fashion has led to an increase in the amount of clothing being discarded after only a few wears. This disposable culture is fueled by the constant influx of new trends and the low quality of many fast fashion garments, which are designed to be worn for a short period before being replaced. The result is a growing mountain of textile waste that ends up in landfills, where it can take decades or even centuries to decompose.

The social impact of fast fashion is equally alarming. The industry's relentless pursuit of low costs and high profits has led to the exploitation of workers in developing countries. Many garment workers are paid poverty wages and forced to work in dangerous and unhealthy conditions. They often lack basic labor rights, such as the right to organize and bargain collectively, and are vulnerable to abuse and exploitation by their employers.

The issue of child labor is also prevalent in the fast fashion industry. In some countries, children as young as ten years old are employed in garment factories, where they are exposed to hazardous working conditions and denied the opportunity to attend school and pursue their education. The use of child labor not only violates international labor standards but also perpetuates poverty and inequality in these communities.

The environmental and social costs of fast fashion are not limited to the countries where the clothing is produced. The transportation of clothing from factories to stores and consumers around the world has a significant environmental impact, as it contributes to greenhouse gas emissions and air pollution. Additionally, the disposal of unwanted clothing in landfills can also have negative environmental consequences, as it contributes to the release of methane, a potent greenhouse gas.

The fast fashion industry's impact on consumer behavior is also a cause for concern. The constant influx of new trends and the pressure to keep up with the latest styles have created a culture of overconsumption. Consumers are encouraged to buy more clothes than they need, often discarding perfectly good garments in favor of the latest trends. This throwaway culture not only fuels the demand for fast fashion but also contributes to the growing problem of textile waste.

Despite the growing awareness of the negative consequences of fast fashion, the industry continues to thrive. The allure of cheap and trendy clothing is difficult to resist, and many consumers are unaware of the hidden costs associated with their purchases. However, there is a growing movement towards sustainable and ethical fashion, as more and more consumers are seeking out brands that prioritize social and environmental responsibility.

There are a number of ways in which consumers can make more sustainable fashion choices. One option is to buy less clothing and invest in higher quality garments that will last longer. Another option is to buy secondhand or vintage clothing, which not only reduces waste but also offers a unique and individual style. Consumers can also support ethical fashion brands that prioritize fair labor practices and sustainable materials.

In addition to individual action, there is a need for systemic change in the fashion industry. Governments and international organizations can play a role in promoting sustainable practices and holding companies accountable for their social and environmental impact. Consumers can also use their voices and wallets to demand change from the industry, by supporting brands that prioritize sustainability and boycotting those that engage in unethical practices.

The hidden cost of fast fashion is a complex issue with far-reaching consequences. The environmental and social impact of the industry is a cause for concern, and there is a growing need for more sustainable and ethical practices. By making informed choices and supporting sustainable brands, consumers can play a role in creating a more responsible and equitable fashion industry.

The future of fashion lies in embracing sustainability and ethical practices. This means moving away from the disposable culture of fast fashion and towards a more circular model, where clothing is designed to last longer and be reused or recycled at the end of its life. It also means prioritizing fair labor practices and ensuring that garment workers are paid a living wage and work in safe and healthy conditions.

ᗘᗘᗘ

Fast fashion's allure hides a devastating truth: environmental ruin and human exploitation. We must embrace sustainable style, where every garment tells a story of ethical creation and conscious consumption. Let your wardrobe reflect your values, not the industry's greed.

TWO

SUSTAINABLE STYLE: DEFINING ETHICAL AND ECO-FRIENDLY FASHION

In a world grappling with the consequences of overconsumption and environmental degradation, the concept of sustainable style has emerged as a beacon of hope for the fashion industry. It represents a paradigm shift away from the fleeting trends and disposable culture of fast fashion, towards a more conscious and responsible approach to clothing. Sustainable style, also known as ethical or eco-friendly fashion, encompasses a wide range of practices and considerations that aim to minimize the negative impact of fashion on the environment and society.

At its core, sustainable style is about making informed choices about the clothes we wear. It involves considering the entire lifecycle of a garment, from the sourcing of raw materials and the manufacturing process to the transportation and disposal of the product. It also involves supporting brands and designers who prioritize ethical practices, such as fair labor conditions, transparency in their supply chains, and the use of sustainable materials.

One of the key aspects of sustainable style is the use of eco-friendly materials. This means choosing fabrics that have a lower environmental impact than conventional materials, such as organic cotton, hemp, linen, bamboo, and recycled fibers. These materials are often grown or produced using less water, energy, and chemicals than their conventional counterparts, and they may also be biodegradable or recyclable at the end of their life.

Another important aspect of sustainable style is the concept of slow fashion. This movement encourages consumers to buy fewer clothes, but of higher quality, that will last longer and can be worn for multiple seasons. Slow fashion also emphasizes timeless styles and classic designs that are not dictated by fleeting trends, thus reducing the need to constantly update one's wardrobe.

Circular fashion is another key principle of sustainable style. This approach aims to close the loop on textile waste by designing garments that can be easily repaired, reused, or recycled at the end of their life. This involves using materials that are durable and long-lasting, as well as designing for disassembly, so that garments can be easily taken apart and their components reused or recycled.

Fair trade fashion is also an important consideration for sustainable style. This means supporting brands and designers who ensure that their workers are paid fair wages, work in safe and healthy conditions, and have the right to organize and bargain collectively. Fair trade fashion also promotes transparency in supply chains, so that consumers can be confident that the clothes they buy are not produced through exploitation.

In addition to these core principles, sustainable style also encompasses a range of other practices and considerations. These may include supporting local designers and artisans, choosing clothing that is made to last, repairing and mending clothes instead of discarding them, and donating unwanted clothing to charity or recycling programs.

The benefits of sustainable style are numerous. By choosing eco-friendly materials and supporting ethical brands, consumers can help to reduce the environmental impact of the fashion industry. This can include reducing greenhouse gas emissions, water pollution, and waste generation. Sustainable style can also help to promote social justice and improve the lives of garment workers around the world.

By choosing sustainable style, consumers can also make a positive impact on their own lives. By investing in high-quality garments that are made to last, they can save money in the long run and reduce the clutter in their closets. Sustainable style can also help to foster a more mindful and intentional approach to fashion, where consumers think more carefully about the clothes they buy and the impact they have.

Of course, there are also challenges associated with sustainable style. One of the main challenges is the cost. Sustainable materials and ethical production practices can be more expensive than conventional methods, which can make sustainable fashion less accessible to some consumers. However, it is important to remember that the true cost of fast fashion is not reflected in the price tag, as it includes the environmental and social costs that are often hidden from view.

Another challenge is the lack of awareness and understanding of sustainable style. Many consumers are not aware of the negative impact of fast fashion or the alternatives that are available. There is a need for more education and awareness-raising campaigns to inform consumers about the importance of sustainable fashion and the choices they can make.

Despite these challenges, the sustainable style movement is gaining momentum. More and more consumers are demanding sustainable and ethical options, and brands and designers are responding to this demand by creating more sustainable collections. There is also a growing network of organizations and initiatives that are working to promote sustainable fashion and support ethical practices in the industry.

The future of fashion lies in embracing sustainable style. This means moving away from the disposable culture of fast fashion and towards a more circular model, where clothing is designed to last longer and be reused or recycled at the end of its life. It also means prioritizing ethical practices, such as fair labor conditions and transparency in supply chains. By choosing sustainable style, consumers can play a role in creating a more responsible and equitable fashion industry.

Sustainable style is not just a trend; it is a movement towards a more conscious and responsible approach to fashion. It is about making informed choices about the clothes we wear and the impact they have on the environment and society. By choosing eco-friendly materials, supporting ethical brands, and embracing slow and circular fashion, we can all contribute to a more sustainable future for the fashion industry and the planet.

ᐳᐳᐳ

Mindful consumption is not about deprivation; it's about intention. Curate a closet filled with pieces you truly love, that resonate with your style and values. When you cherish each item, you naturally consume less and reduce waste.

THREE

MINDFUL CONSUMPTION: CURATING A CONSCIOUS CLOSET

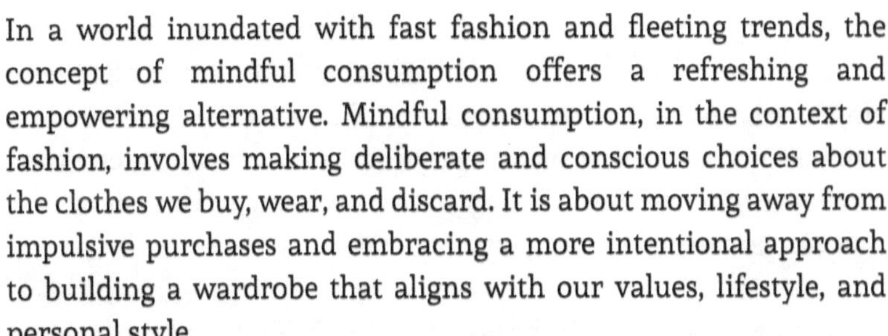

In a world inundated with fast fashion and fleeting trends, the concept of mindful consumption offers a refreshing and empowering alternative. Mindful consumption, in the context of fashion, involves making deliberate and conscious choices about the clothes we buy, wear, and discard. It is about moving away from impulsive purchases and embracing a more intentional approach to building a wardrobe that aligns with our values, lifestyle, and personal style.

At its core, mindful consumption is about recognizing that our clothing choices have a significant impact on the environment, society, and ourselves. It involves considering the entire lifecycle of a garment, from the sourcing of raw materials and the manufacturing process to the transportation and disposal of the product. It also involves questioning the societal norms and marketing messages that encourage us to constantly consume new clothing, regardless of our actual needs or the impact of our choices.

One of the key aspects of mindful consumption is cultivating awareness. This means paying attention to our shopping habits, our motivations for buying clothes, and the impact of our choices on the environment and society. It involves asking ourselves questions like: Do I really need this item? Will I wear it multiple times? Is it made from sustainable materials? Was it produced ethically? By taking the time to consider these questions, we can start to make more informed and conscious decisions about our clothing purchases.

Another important aspect of mindful consumption is practicing gratitude. This means appreciating the clothes we already have and finding ways to maximize their use. It involves taking care of our garments, repairing them when necessary, and finding creative ways to style them for different occasions. It also involves resisting the urge to constantly buy new clothes and instead focusing on the value and versatility of the pieces we already own.

Building a conscious closet is a key component of mindful consumption. This involves curating a wardrobe that is filled with clothes that we love, that fit well, and that we will wear for years to come. It also involves prioritizing quality over quantity, choosing timeless styles over fleeting trends, and investing in versatile pieces that can be dressed up or down.

Creating a capsule wardrobe is one way to build a conscious closet. A capsule wardrobe is a small collection of essential pieces that can be mixed and matched to create a variety of outfits. This approach not only simplifies our wardrobes but also encourages us to be more creative with our styling and to appreciate the versatility of our clothes.

Thrifting and secondhand shopping are also great ways to practice mindful consumption. By buying pre-loved clothes, we not only reduce waste and extend the life of garments, but we also discover unique and one-of-a-kind pieces that add character to our wardrobes. Additionally, supporting sustainable and ethical brands is another important aspect of mindful consumption. By choosing brands that prioritize fair labor practices, sustainable materials, and transparent supply chains, we can use our purchasing power to promote positive change in the fashion industry.

Mindful consumption also involves considering the environmental impact of our clothing choices. This means choosing fabrics that are made from sustainable materials, such as organic cotton, hemp, linen, bamboo, and recycled fibers. It also means being mindful of the water and energy used in the production of our clothes and choosing brands that prioritize sustainable manufacturing processes.

In addition to the environmental and social impact, mindful consumption also has a positive impact on our mental and emotional well-being. By making conscious choices about the clothes we wear, we can cultivate a deeper sense of connection to our wardrobes and our personal style. We can also reduce the stress and anxiety that can come from constantly chasing trends and feeling the pressure to keep up with the latest fashion.

Mindful consumption is not about deprivation or sacrificing style. It is about making choices that align with our values and priorities. It is about finding joy and satisfaction in the clothes we already have and investing in pieces that we will cherish for years to come. It is about embracing a more conscious and intentional approach to fashion that benefits not only ourselves but also the planet and the people who make our clothes.

The journey towards mindful consumption may not be easy, as it requires us to challenge societal norms and question our own habits and beliefs. However, the rewards are immense. By cultivating awareness, gratitude, and intentionality in our clothing choices, we can not only transform our wardrobes but also our relationship with fashion. We can break free from the cycle of overconsumption and discover a more fulfilling and sustainable way of dressing.

❧❧❧

Sustainable materials are the building blocks of a responsible wardrobe. Embrace organic cotton, hemp, linen, and recycled fibers – fabrics that tread lightly on the Earth. Let your clothes be a testament to your commitment to a healthier planet.

FOUR

Fabric of the Future: Exploring Sustainable Materials

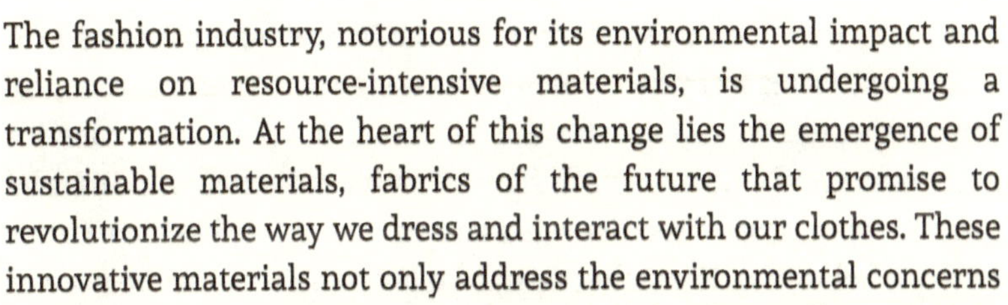

The fashion industry, notorious for its environmental impact and reliance on resource-intensive materials, is undergoing a transformation. At the heart of this change lies the emergence of sustainable materials, fabrics of the future that promise to revolutionize the way we dress and interact with our clothes. These innovative materials not only address the environmental concerns associated with traditional textiles but also offer exciting possibilities for design, performance, and functionality.

One of the most promising categories of sustainable materials is natural fibers. These fibers, derived from plants or animals, have a long history of use in textiles and are known for their biodegradability and renewability. Organic cotton, for example, is grown without the use of harmful pesticides and fertilizers, making it a more environmentally friendly alternative to conventional cotton. Hemp, a versatile fiber known for its strength and durability, requires minimal water and pesticides to grow, making it a sustainable choice for a variety of textile applications. Linen, derived from the flax plant, is another sustainable option that is known for its breathability and natural antibacterial properties.

In addition to these well-known natural fibers, there is a growing interest in innovative materials derived from unexpected sources. One such example is Piñatex, a leather-like material made from pineapple leaf fibers. This innovative material offers a cruelty-free and sustainable alternative to traditional leather, and it has already been adopted by several fashion brands. Another exciting development is the use of orange fiber, a byproduct of the citrus juice industry, to create sustainable textiles. This material not only reduces waste but also offers unique properties such as a soft hand feel and natural antimicrobial properties.

Recycled fibers are another important category of sustainable materials. These fibers are made from post-consumer or post-industrial waste, such as plastic bottles, fishing nets, and textile scraps. By diverting waste from landfills and reducing the need for virgin materials, recycled fibers offer a significant environmental advantage. Recycled polyester, for example, is a popular choice for activewear and outdoor clothing due to its moisture-wicking and quick-drying properties. Recycled cotton, made from textile scraps and used clothing, is another sustainable option that can be used to create a variety of garments.

One of the most exciting developments in sustainable materials is the emergence of bio-based fibers. These fibers are derived from renewable resources, such as algae, corn, and soybeans, and they offer a promising alternative to petroleum-based fibers. One example is Sorona, a bio-based fiber made from corn sugar. This fiber is known for its softness, stretch, and resistance to wrinkles, making it a versatile choice for a variety of garments. Another example is SeaCell, a fiber made from seaweed and wood pulp. This fiber is naturally breathable and moisture-wicking, and it is also said to have anti-inflammatory properties.

In addition to their environmental benefits, sustainable materials also offer exciting possibilities for design and functionality. Many of these materials have unique properties that can be leveraged to create innovative and high-performance garments. For example, some sustainable materials are naturally antimicrobial, meaning they can help to prevent the growth of bacteria and odor. Others are naturally water-resistant or quick-drying, making them ideal for outdoor and activewear.

The development of sustainable materials is not without its challenges. One of the main challenges is the cost. Sustainable materials can be more expensive to produce than conventional materials, which can make them less accessible to some consumers. However, as the demand for sustainable fashion grows, the cost of these materials is likely to decrease.

Another challenge is the need for more research and development. While there are many promising sustainable materials available, there is still much work to be done in terms of developing new materials and improving existing ones. This includes finding ways to make sustainable materials more durable, affordable, and accessible to a wider range of consumers.

Despite these challenges, the future of fashion is bright. The emergence of sustainable materials is a testament to the industry's commitment to innovation and sustainability. As more and more designers and brands embrace these materials, we can expect to see a wider range of sustainable clothing options on the market. This will not only help to reduce the environmental impact of the fashion industry but also inspire a new generation of consumers to make more conscious and responsible choices about the clothes they wear.

The fabrics of the future are not just about sustainability; they are also about innovation, design, and functionality. By embracing these materials, the fashion industry can create a more sustainable and equitable future for all.

Slow down, savor quality, and reject the fleeting trends of fast fashion. Invest in timeless pieces that transcend seasons and trends. Your wardrobe should reflect your personal style, not the dictates of the industry.

FIVE

Slow Fashion Movement: Embracing Quality Over Quantity

In a world inundated with fleeting trends and disposable fashion, the slow fashion movement emerges as a refreshing antidote, offering a more conscious and sustainable approach to clothing consumption. Unlike fast fashion, which thrives on rapid production cycles and ever-changing styles, slow fashion embraces quality, craftsmanship, and timeless design. It encourages consumers to invest in well-made garments that will last for years, rather than succumbing to the allure of cheap and trendy clothes that are quickly discarded.

At its core, the slow fashion movement is about challenging the prevailing culture of overconsumption and disposability that has become synonymous with the fashion industry. It advocates for a return to traditional values of quality, durability, and craftsmanship, where garments are seen as investments rather than disposable items. By choosing quality over quantity, consumers can not only reduce their environmental impact but also cultivate a more meaningful relationship with their clothes.

One of the key principles of slow fashion is the emphasis on transparency and ethical production. Slow fashion brands often prioritize transparency in their supply chains, allowing consumers to trace the origins of their garments and ensuring that they are produced under fair and safe working conditions. This not only empowers consumers to make informed choices but also supports the livelihoods of garment workers and promotes social justice in the fashion industry.

Another important aspect of slow fashion is the use of sustainable materials. Many slow fashion brands prioritize the use of organic, recycled, or upcycled materials, as well as natural fibers like cotton, linen, and wool. These materials are not only better for the environment but also tend to be more durable and long-lasting than synthetic materials often used in fast fashion.

Slow fashion also embraces the concept of timeless design. Instead of chasing after fleeting trends, slow fashion brands focus on creating classic and versatile pieces that can be worn for years to come. This not only reduces the need to constantly update one's wardrobe but also encourages a more personal and individual style.

The slow fashion movement is not just about buying less and choosing quality over quantity. It is also about changing our relationship with clothes. It encourages us to appreciate the craftsmanship and story behind each garment, to take care of our clothes and repair them when needed, and to cherish the memories and experiences associated with each piece.

The benefits of embracing slow fashion are numerous. By investing in quality garments that are made to last, we can reduce our environmental impact by minimizing waste and conserving resources. We can also support ethical production practices and promote fair labor conditions for garment workers. Additionally, slow fashion can help us to develop a more personal and unique style, as we move away from mass-produced trends and embrace timeless pieces that reflect our individuality.

While the slow fashion movement is gaining momentum, there are still challenges to overcome. One of the main challenges is the perception that slow fashion is expensive. While it is true that high-quality garments often come with a higher price tag, it is important to remember that they are investments that will last for years, rather than disposable items that need to be replaced every season. Additionally, there are many affordable slow fashion brands that offer stylish and sustainable options at accessible prices.

Another challenge is the accessibility of slow fashion. While there are many online and brick-and-mortar stores that offer slow fashion brands, they may not be readily available in all areas. However, the rise of e-commerce and the growing demand for sustainable fashion are making slow fashion more accessible than ever before.

The slow fashion movement is more than just a trend; it is a cultural shift towards a more conscious and responsible approach to fashion consumption. By embracing quality over quantity, supporting ethical production, and cherishing our clothes, we can create a more sustainable and equitable fashion industry. Slow fashion offers a path towards a more fulfilling and meaningful relationship with our clothes, one that celebrates craftsmanship, individuality, and sustainability.

As consumers, we have the power to drive change in the fashion industry by choosing to support slow fashion brands and rejecting the unsustainable practices of fast fashion. By embracing the slow fashion movement, we can not only transform our wardrobes but also contribute to a more sustainable and equitable future for the planet and its people.

❧❧❧

Circular fashion is not just a concept; it's a necessity. Let's close the loop on textile waste by embracing reuse, repair, and recycling. Every garment has the potential for multiple lives; let's give them the chance to shine again.

SIX

CIRCULAR FASHION: CLOSING THE LOOP ON TEXTILE WASTE

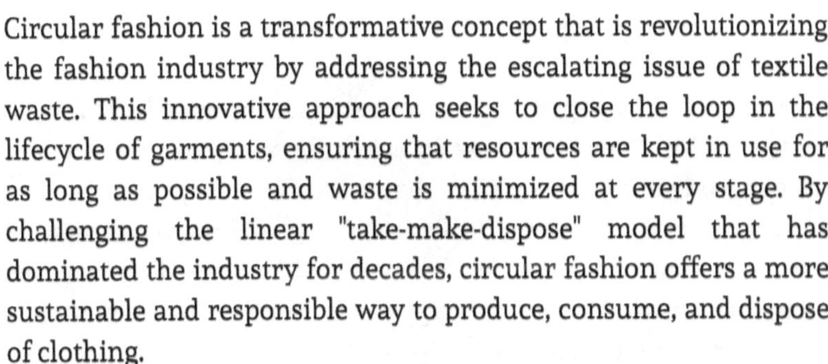

Circular fashion is a transformative concept that is revolutionizing the fashion industry by addressing the escalating issue of textile waste. This innovative approach seeks to close the loop in the lifecycle of garments, ensuring that resources are kept in use for as long as possible and waste is minimized at every stage. By challenging the linear "take-make-dispose" model that has dominated the industry for decades, circular fashion offers a more sustainable and responsible way to produce, consume, and dispose of clothing.

At its core, circular fashion is based on the principles of the circular economy, a regenerative system that aims to eliminate waste and pollution by keeping products and materials in use through reuse, repair, refurbishment, and recycling. In the context of fashion, this means designing clothes with durability, longevity, and recyclability in mind, as well as creating systems that facilitate the collection, sorting, and processing of used clothing.

The current linear model of fashion production and consumption has led to a massive accumulation of textile waste. According to the Ellen MacArthur Foundation, an estimated $500 billion worth of value is lost each year due to clothing underutilization and the lack of recycling. This waste not only represents a significant economic loss but also has a devastating impact on the environment. The production of textiles requires vast amounts of water, energy, and chemicals, and the disposal of clothing in landfills contributes to greenhouse gas emissions and soil contamination.

Circular fashion aims to address this problem by creating a closed-loop system where garments are designed to be reused, repaired, or recycled at the end of their life. This involves a shift in mindset from "fast fashion" to "slow fashion," where garments are valued for their quality and durability rather than their trendiness. It also requires a collaborative effort from designers, manufacturers, retailers, consumers, and policymakers to create the infrastructure and systems needed to support a circular economy for fashion.

One of the key strategies in circular fashion is the use of sustainable materials. This involves using recycled fibers, organic cotton, and other eco-friendly materials that can be easily recycled or biodegraded at the end of their life. It also involves designing garments that can be easily disassembled for recycling, such as using detachable buttons and zippers or avoiding mixed materials that are difficult to separate.

Another important aspect of circular fashion is the promotion of reuse and repair. This can be achieved through initiatives such as clothing swaps, repair workshops, and online platforms that connect people who want to buy and sell secondhand clothes. By extending the lifespan of garments, reuse and repair can significantly reduce the demand for new clothing and the associated environmental impact.

Recycling is another crucial component of circular fashion. However, textile recycling is a complex process that requires specialized technologies and infrastructure. One of the challenges is separating different types of fibers and materials, which can be difficult and costly. Additionally, the quality of recycled fibers can vary, which can limit their use in high-quality garments. Nevertheless, advances in textile recycling technologies are making it possible to create high-quality yarns and fabrics from recycled materials, paving the way for a more circular fashion industry.

The transition to circular fashion also requires a change in consumer behavior. Consumers need to be educated about the benefits of buying less and choosing quality over quantity. They also need to be aware of the environmental and social impact of their clothing choices and the options available for disposing of unwanted garments responsibly.

Policymakers also have a role to play in promoting circular fashion. This can include introducing legislation that incentivizes sustainable practices, such as extended producer responsibility (EPR) schemes, where manufacturers are responsible for the collection and recycling of their products. It can also involve supporting research and development of new recycling technologies and creating a favorable environment for businesses that adopt circular models.

The benefits of circular fashion are numerous. By reducing waste, conserving resources, and promoting sustainable practices, circular fashion can help to mitigate the environmental impact of the fashion industry. It can also create new economic opportunities, such as jobs in recycling and repair, and foster innovation in design and manufacturing. Additionally, circular fashion can empower consumers to make more conscious and responsible choices about their clothing, leading to a more sustainable and equitable fashion system.

The transition to circular fashion is not without its challenges. It requires a significant shift in mindset and practice across the entire fashion industry, from designers and manufacturers to retailers and consumers. It also requires investment in new technologies and infrastructure, as well as supportive policies and regulations. However, the potential benefits of circular fashion are too significant to ignore. By embracing this transformative approach, we can create a fashion industry that is not only environmentally sustainable but also socially responsible and economically viable.

ᗰᗰᗰ

Fair trade fashion is about justice and dignity for those who create our clothes. Support brands that prioritize fair wages, safe working conditions, and community development. Your choices can empower workers and transform lives.

SEVEN

Fair Trade Fashion: Supporting Ethical Production

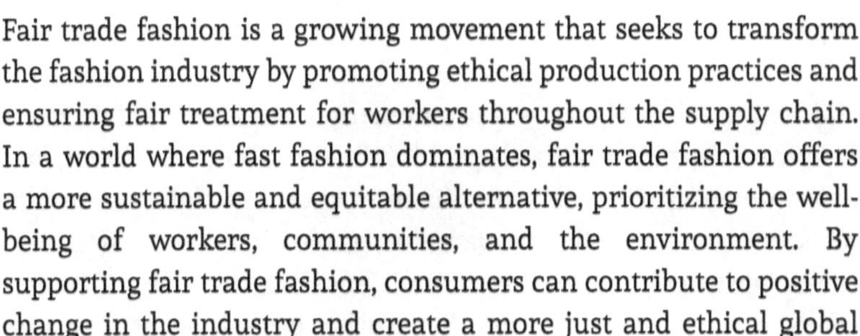

Fair trade fashion is a growing movement that seeks to transform the fashion industry by promoting ethical production practices and ensuring fair treatment for workers throughout the supply chain. In a world where fast fashion dominates, fair trade fashion offers a more sustainable and equitable alternative, prioritizing the well-being of workers, communities, and the environment. By supporting fair trade fashion, consumers can contribute to positive change in the industry and create a more just and ethical global economy.

At its core, fair trade fashion is about ensuring that the people who make our clothes are treated with dignity and respect. It involves paying fair wages, providing safe working conditions, and upholding labor rights, such as the right to freedom of association and collective bargaining. Fair trade fashion also goes beyond the workplace, investing in community development projects that improve the lives of workers and their families.

One of the key principles of fair trade fashion is the payment of a fair price. This means paying farmers and producers a price that covers the cost of sustainable production and allows them to earn a decent living. Fair trade organizations often set minimum prices for certain commodities, such as cotton, to ensure that farmers receive a fair return for their labor. Additionally, fair trade premiums are often paid on top of the fair price, which are invested in community development projects chosen by the farmers and workers themselves.

Another important aspect of fair trade fashion is the provision of safe and healthy working conditions. Fair trade standards require that workplaces are free from hazards, such as exposure to harmful chemicals and dangerous machinery. They also require that workers have access to clean water, sanitation facilities, and healthcare. Additionally, fair trade organizations often provide training on health and safety issues to workers and their supervisors.

Upholding labor rights is a fundamental principle of fair trade fashion. Fair trade standards prohibit forced labor, child labor, and discrimination. They also guarantee workers the right to freedom of association and collective bargaining, allowing them to negotiate for better wages and working conditions. Fair trade organizations often work with unions and other worker organizations to ensure that workers' rights are respected and upheld.

Fair trade fashion also recognizes the importance of environmental sustainability. Fair trade standards encourage the use of environmentally friendly practices, such as organic farming, water conservation, and the reduction of waste. They also promote the use of renewable energy sources and the minimization of greenhouse gas emissions. By supporting fair trade fashion, consumers can contribute to a more sustainable and environmentally responsible fashion industry.

Beyond the workplace, fair trade fashion invests in community development projects that improve the lives of workers and their families. These projects can include building schools, providing healthcare, supporting women's empowerment initiatives, and promoting sustainable agriculture. By investing in community development, fair trade fashion not only improves the livelihoods of workers but also strengthens the social fabric of their communities.

The benefits of fair trade fashion are numerous. For workers, it means fair wages, safe working conditions, and the right to organize and bargain collectively. For communities, it means access to education, healthcare, and other essential services. For the environment, it means sustainable production practices that protect natural resources and reduce pollution. And for consumers, it means the peace of mind of knowing that their clothes were made ethically and responsibly.

Despite the growing demand for fair trade fashion, there are still challenges to overcome. One of the main challenges is the lack of awareness among consumers. Many people are still not aware of the social and environmental impact of their clothing choices, or of the fair trade alternative. There is a need for more education and awareness-raising campaigns to inform consumers about the importance of fair trade fashion and the choices they can make.

Another challenge is the higher cost of fair trade fashion. Fair trade products often cost more than conventional products because they reflect the true cost of production, including fair wages and environmental protection. However, it is important to remember that the lower price of conventional products often comes at the expense of workers and the environment. By supporting fair trade fashion, consumers are investing in a more sustainable and equitable future for the fashion industry.

The fair trade fashion movement is gaining momentum as more and more consumers become aware of the social and environmental impact of their clothing choices. By supporting fair trade fashion, we can create a more just and ethical global economy, where workers are treated with dignity and respect, communities thrive, and the environment is protected.

ϷϷϷ

Secondhand chic is not just about saving money; it's about embracing individuality and reducing waste. Thrifting and vintage shopping offer a treasure trove of unique finds that tell stories of the past. Let your style be a reflection of your values and your unique journey.

EIGHT

SECONDHAND CHIC: THE JOY OF THRIFTING AND VINTAGE

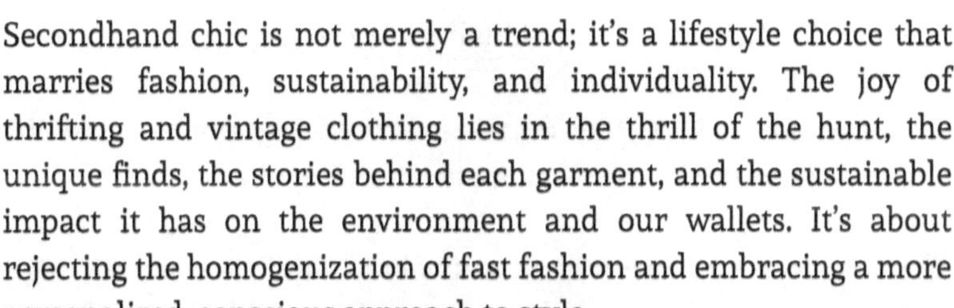

Secondhand chic is not merely a trend; it's a lifestyle choice that marries fashion, sustainability, and individuality. The joy of thrifting and vintage clothing lies in the thrill of the hunt, the unique finds, the stories behind each garment, and the sustainable impact it has on the environment and our wallets. It's about rejecting the homogenization of fast fashion and embracing a more personalized, conscious approach to style.

Thrifting, often synonymous with secondhand shopping, involves purchasing pre-owned clothing and accessories from thrift stores, consignment shops, or online platforms.

Vintage clothing, on the other hand, refers to garments typically from a previous era, usually 20 years or older, that have withstood the test of time and become classics. Both thrifting and vintage shopping offer a treasure trove of unique and affordable finds that can elevate any wardrobe.

The allure of secondhand chic lies in the thrill of the hunt. Thrift stores are like treasure chests filled with hidden gems waiting to be discovered. Each item has a story to tell, a past life that adds to its charm and character. Unlike the predictable offerings of fast fashion, thrifting allows for serendipitous discoveries, fostering a sense of adventure and excitement.

Moreover, secondhand clothing offers a unique opportunity for self-expression. With a vast array of styles, eras, and brands to choose from, thrifting allows individuals to curate a wardrobe that truly reflects their personality and taste.

It's about breaking free from the mold of mass-produced fashion and embracing individuality. Vintage pieces, in particular, can add a touch of nostalgia and sophistication to any outfit, making a statement that goes beyond the latest trends.

Beyond the thrill and individuality, secondhand chic is also a sustainable and ethical choice. By giving new life to pre-owned clothing, we reduce the demand for new garments, thereby decreasing the environmental impact of the fashion industry.

The production of new clothing involves significant water usage, energy consumption, and the release of harmful chemicals and greenhouse gases. By choosing secondhand, we can help to mitigate these environmental impacts and contribute to a more sustainable future.

Thrifting also has a positive social impact. Many thrift stores are run by charitable organizations, and the proceeds from sales often go towards supporting local communities. Additionally, by buying secondhand, we support a circular economy where resources are kept in use for as long as possible, reducing waste and promoting sustainability.

Another compelling reason to embrace secondhand chic is the affordability. Thrift stores offer a vast array of clothing and accessories at a fraction of the price of new items. This allows fashion enthusiasts to experiment with different styles, expand their wardrobes, and stay on top of trends without breaking the bank. Vintage pieces, often made with higher quality materials and craftsmanship than modern fast fashion, can be found at reasonable prices, making them a worthwhile investment.

However, thrifting and vintage shopping require a different approach than traditional retail shopping. It requires patience, a keen eye for detail, and a willingness to explore.

It's important to be open-minded and willing to try on different styles and sizes. It's also crucial to inspect items carefully for any flaws or damages before purchasing.

With the rise of online platforms dedicated to secondhand and vintage clothing, the accessibility and convenience of thrifting have increased significantly. These platforms offer a curated selection of pre-owned items, often with detailed descriptions and photographs, making it easier for shoppers to find what they're looking for.

Additionally, online platforms often have search filters and size guides, making the browsing and purchasing process more efficient.

Secondhand chic is not just about shopping; it's a community. It's about connecting with fellow thrifters, sharing tips and tricks, and celebrating the joy of finding unique treasures.

Social media platforms have become hubs for secondhand fashion enthusiasts, with hashtags like #thrifting and #vintagefashion showcasing the creativity and diversity of this movement.

As the environmental and social impact of fast fashion becomes increasingly apparent, the allure of secondhand chic continues to grow. More and more consumers are realizing the benefits of thrifting and vintage shopping, both for themselves and the planet.

By embracing secondhand chic, we can redefine our relationship with fashion, prioritize sustainability, and express our individuality through unique and timeless pieces.

ppp

Unleash your creativity and transform old clothes into new treasures. DIY and upcycling empower you to take ownership of your wardrobe and express your individuality. Let your creativity bloom as you breathe new life into forgotten garments.

NINE

DIY AND UPCYCLING: BREATHING NEW LIFE INTO OLD CLOTHES

In a world grappling with the environmental consequences of fast fashion and the ever-growing mountains of textile waste, the art of DIY (Do It Yourself) and upcycling emerges as a creative and sustainable solution. DIY and upcycling breathe new life into old clothes, transforming them into unique and personalized pieces that reflect individual style and reduce environmental impact. This approach not only fosters creativity and resourcefulness but also challenges the throwaway culture that has plagued the fashion industry.

DIY fashion is about taking ownership of our clothes and expressing our individuality through creativity. It involves repurposing old garments, altering their fit or style, and adding personal touches to create something new and unique.

It can be as simple as sewing on a patch, adding embellishments, or dyeing a faded garment. Or it can involve more complex projects like transforming a dress into a skirt or a pair of jeans into shorts. The possibilities are endless, and the only limit is one's imagination.

Upcycling, on the other hand, is about transforming discarded materials into something of higher quality or value. In the context of fashion, it involves taking old clothes, fabrics, or other materials and turning them into new garments or accessories.

This can be done by cutting up old t-shirts to create a patchwork quilt, transforming old jeans into a trendy tote bag, or repurposing vintage scarves into stylish headbands. Upcycling not only reduces waste but also adds a unique and personal touch to one's wardrobe.

The DIY and upcycling movement is gaining momentum as more and more people become aware of the environmental and social impact of fast fashion. By embracing these practices, we can reduce our reliance on new clothing production, which consumes vast amounts of resources and contributes to pollution and waste.

DIY and upcycling also offer a more sustainable and affordable way to express our personal style, as we can create unique pieces that reflect our individuality without breaking the bank.

One of the most appealing aspects of DIY and upcycling is the sense of empowerment it provides. By learning new skills and techniques, we can take control of our wardrobes and create clothes that truly reflect our personal style.

We can also develop a deeper appreciation for the craftsmanship and effort that goes into making clothes, as we learn to mend and alter our garments ourselves.

The DIY and upcycling community is thriving, with a wealth of resources available online and offline to inspire and guide aspiring creators. Websites, blogs, and social media platforms are filled with tutorials, tips, and ideas for upcycling projects. There are also numerous workshops, classes, and events dedicated to teaching people how to sew, knit, crochet, and other crafts that can be used to transform old clothes into new treasures.

In addition to the environmental and personal benefits, DIY and upcycling can also have a positive social impact. By sharing our skills and knowledge with others, we can empower them to create their own unique pieces and reduce their reliance on fast fashion.

We can also support local artisans and businesses that specialize in upcycled and handmade goods, contributing to a more sustainable and equitable economy.

However, DIY and upcycling are not without their challenges. One of the main challenges is the time and effort required to learn new skills and complete projects. It can be intimidating for beginners to start a DIY project, especially if they lack the necessary tools and materials.

However, with the abundance of resources available online and offline, it has never been easier to learn the basics and get started.

Another challenge is the perception that DIY and upcycled clothes are not as fashionable or desirable as new clothes. However, this perception is rapidly changing, as more and more designers and brands embrace upcycling and incorporate sustainable practices into their collections.

Upcycled fashion is now seen as a creative and innovative way to express oneself, and it is gaining popularity among fashion-conscious consumers who are looking for unique and sustainable alternatives to fast fashion.

The DIY and upcycling movement is not just about creating new clothes; it is about transforming our relationship with fashion. It is about moving away from the throwaway culture of fast fashion and embracing a more sustainable and mindful approach to clothing consumption. By learning to mend, alter, and upcycle our clothes, we can extend their lifespan, reduce waste, and express our individuality in a way that is both creative and sustainable.

PPP

A capsule wardrobe is a minimalist's dream, a curated collection of essential pieces that can be mixed and matched to create endless possibilities. Embrace simplicity, functionality, and versatility, and free yourself from the clutter of excess.

TEN

CAPSULE WARDROBE: BUILDING A VERSATILE AND SUSTAINABLE CLOSET

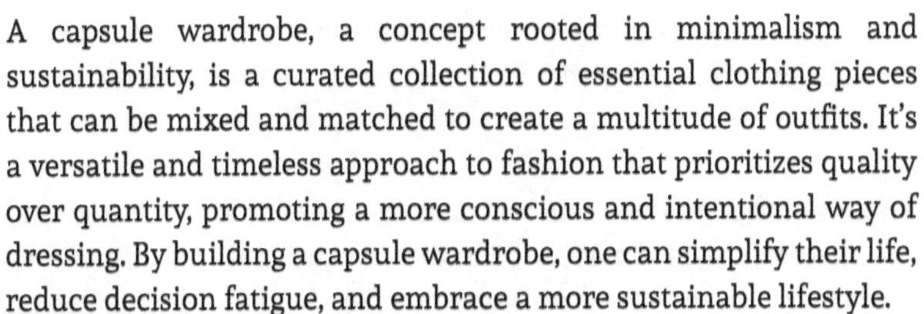

A capsule wardrobe, a concept rooted in minimalism and sustainability, is a curated collection of essential clothing pieces that can be mixed and matched to create a multitude of outfits. It's a versatile and timeless approach to fashion that prioritizes quality over quantity, promoting a more conscious and intentional way of dressing. By building a capsule wardrobe, one can simplify their life, reduce decision fatigue, and embrace a more sustainable lifestyle.

The concept of a capsule wardrobe was first introduced in the 1970s by Susie Faux, the owner of a London boutique called "Wardrobe." Faux advocated for a minimalist approach to fashion, suggesting that a carefully curated collection of essential pieces could create a multitude of outfits, eliminating the need for a large and overflowing wardrobe.

The concept gained popularity again in the 1980s when American designer Donna Karan launched her "Seven Easy Pieces" collection, which consisted of seven interchangeable items that could be dressed up or down for any occasion.

Today, the capsule wardrobe has evolved into a global movement, embraced by people from all walks of life who are seeking a more simplified and sustainable approach to fashion. It has become a symbol of conscious consumerism, rejecting the fast fashion cycle of constant consumption and disposability.

Building a capsule wardrobe starts with decluttering and simplifying your existing wardrobe. This involves taking a critical look at your clothes and identifying the pieces that you truly love, wear regularly, and that fit well.

It's about letting go of items that no longer serve you, whether they are worn out, ill-fitting, or simply not your style. This process can be liberating, freeing up space in your closet and your mind.

Once you have decluttered your wardrobe, the next step is to identify the essential pieces that will form the foundation of your capsule wardrobe.

These are the versatile and timeless items that can be mixed and matched to create a variety of outfits for different occasions. The number of pieces in a capsule wardrobe can vary depending on individual preferences and lifestyle, but it typically ranges from 30 to 40 items.

The key to a successful capsule wardrobe is choosing high-quality, versatile pieces that you love. These pieces should be made from durable and sustainable materials that will last for years. They should also be classic and timeless in style, so that they won't go out of fashion quickly. By investing in quality pieces, you will not only save money in the long run but also reduce your environmental impact by minimizing waste.

A typical capsule wardrobe might include a few pairs of jeans in different washes, a few basic t-shirts and blouses, a couple of sweaters or cardigans, a jacket or blazer, a dress or skirt, and a pair of shoes that can be dressed up or down. It's important to choose pieces that reflect your personal style and that can be easily combined to create a variety of looks.

Color palette plays a crucial role in creating a cohesive and versatile capsule wardrobe. Choosing a neutral color palette, such as black, white, grey, and beige, can make it easier to mix and match pieces.

You can then add pops of color with accessories or statement pieces. This approach not only simplifies your outfit choices but also creates a more streamlined and polished look.

Accessories can also play a vital role in a capsule wardrobe. Scarves, belts, jewelry, and bags can be used to elevate a simple outfit and add personality to your look. By choosing a few versatile accessories that can be worn with multiple outfits, you can expand the possibilities of your capsule wardrobe without adding unnecessary clutter.

Building a capsule wardrobe is an ongoing process. As your lifestyle and style evolve, you may need to add or remove pieces from your capsule wardrobe. It's important to regularly assess your wardrobe and ensure that it still serves your needs and reflects your personal style.

A capsule wardrobe is not just about simplifying your closet; it's about embracing a more sustainable and intentional way of dressing.

By choosing quality over quantity, investing in timeless pieces, and prioritizing versatility, you can create a wardrobe that not only makes you feel confident and stylish but also reduces your environmental impact.

ᗝᗝᗝ

Choose ethical brands that prioritize transparency, sustainability, and fair labor practices. Let your purchases support businesses that are making a positive impact on the world. Your choices matter; vote with your wallet.

ELEVEN

ETHICAL BRANDS: DISCOVERING SUSTAINABLE FASHION LABELS

The fashion landscape is undergoing a significant transformation as consumers become more conscious of the environmental and social impact of their clothing choices. This growing awareness has led to an increasing demand for ethical brands, sustainable fashion labels that prioritize transparency, fair labor practices, and eco-friendly materials. Discovering these ethical brands is not just a matter of finding stylish clothes; it's about making a conscious decision to support businesses that align with your values and contribute to a more sustainable and equitable fashion industry.

Ethical brands are defined by their commitment to ethical practices throughout their supply chain. They prioritize transparency, ensuring that consumers have access to information about the origins of their garments, the materials used, and the working conditions of the people who made them. They also prioritize fair labor practices, ensuring that workers are paid fair wages, work in safe and healthy conditions, and have the right to organize and bargain collectively. Additionally, ethical brands strive to minimize their environmental impact by using sustainable materials, reducing waste, and implementing eco-friendly production processes.

The rise of ethical brands is a response to the growing concerns about the social and environmental impact of fast fashion. Fast fashion brands, known for their cheap and trendy clothes, often prioritize profits over people and the planet. They often source their materials from countries with lax labor laws and environmental regulations, where workers are exploited and the environment is polluted. In contrast, ethical brands offer a more responsible and sustainable alternative, proving that fashion can be both stylish and ethical.

Discovering ethical brands can be a rewarding and empowering experience. It allows you to connect with brands that share your values and support businesses that are making a positive impact on the world. There are many ways to discover ethical brands, from online directories and marketplaces to social media and word-of-mouth recommendations.

Online directories and marketplaces, such as Good On You and DoneGood, provide comprehensive information about ethical brands, including their sustainability ratings, certifications, and social impact initiatives. These platforms make it easy to compare and contrast different brands, helping you to make informed choices about where to shop.

Social media platforms, such as Instagram and Pinterest, are also great resources for discovering ethical brands. Many ethical brands use social media to showcase their products, share their stories, and connect with consumers. By following ethical fashion influencers and hashtags, you can stay up-to-date on the latest trends and discover new brands that align with your values.

Word-of-mouth recommendations can also be a valuable way to discover ethical brands. Ask your friends, family, and colleagues about their favorite ethical brands, or join online communities and forums where people share their experiences and recommendations.

When evaluating ethical brands, it's important to look beyond marketing claims and consider their actual practices. Look for brands that are transparent about their supply chain and provide detailed information about their sourcing, manufacturing, and labor practices. Check for certifications from reputable organizations, such as Fairtrade, GOTS (Global Organic Textile Standard), and B Corp, which indicate that a brand meets rigorous social and environmental standards.

It's also important to consider the materials used by ethical brands. Look for brands that use sustainable materials, such as organic cotton, hemp, linen, bamboo, and recycled fibers. These materials have a lower environmental impact than conventional materials, as they require less water, energy, and chemicals to produce.

In addition to these criteria, consider the overall mission and values of the brand. Do they prioritize ethical practices throughout their supply chain? Do they have a transparent and accountable business model? Do they actively engage in social and environmental initiatives? By aligning your values with those of the brands you support, you can create a more positive impact with your purchasing decisions.

The journey of discovering ethical brands is an ongoing one. As the fashion industry evolves, so too will the landscape of ethical brands. New brands are emerging all the time, offering innovative solutions to the challenges facing the fashion industry. By staying informed and engaged, you can continue to discover new and exciting brands that are making a difference.

Supporting ethical brands is more than just a shopping decision; it's a vote for a more sustainable and equitable future for the fashion industry. By choosing to buy from ethical brands, you are sending a message to the industry that you value transparency, fair labor practices, and environmental sustainability. Your choices can influence other consumers, inspire change within the industry, and ultimately contribute to a more ethical and sustainable fashion system.

ᐅᐅᐅ

Greenwashing is a wolf in sheep's clothing, deceiving consumers with false promises of sustainability. Be discerning, research brands thoroughly, and demand transparency. Don't let your good intentions be exploited by misleading claims.

TWELVE

GREENWASHING: IDENTIFYING MISLEADING SUSTAINABILITY CLAIMS

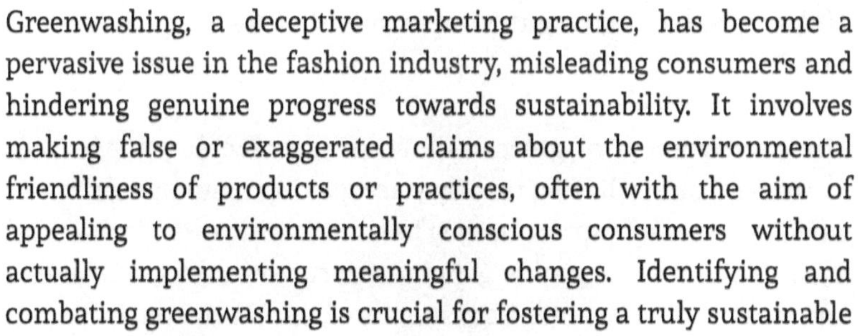

Greenwashing, a deceptive marketing practice, has become a pervasive issue in the fashion industry, misleading consumers and hindering genuine progress towards sustainability. It involves making false or exaggerated claims about the environmental friendliness of products or practices, often with the aim of appealing to environmentally conscious consumers without actually implementing meaningful changes. Identifying and combating greenwashing is crucial for fostering a truly sustainable fashion industry and empowering consumers to make informed choices.

The term "greenwashing" was coined in the 1980s by environmentalist Jay Westerveld, who criticized the hotel industry's practice of encouraging guests to reuse towels as a way to save the environment, while primarily motivated by cost-saving measures. Since then, the term has expanded to encompass a wide range of misleading marketing tactics employed by various industries, including fashion.

In the fashion industry, greenwashing can take many forms. Some common examples include using vague or misleading language, such as "eco-friendly," "sustainable," or "green," without providing concrete evidence or verifiable certifications. Brands may also highlight a single eco-friendly aspect of their product, such as using recycled packaging, while ignoring the environmental impact of the entire production process. Another tactic is to make broad claims about sustainability without providing specific details or measurable goals.

One of the most common forms of greenwashing in the fashion industry is the use of misleading labels and certifications. Some brands create their own labels with eco-friendly sounding names, without adhering to any recognized standards or third-party verification. Others may use legitimate certifications, such as organic cotton or recycled polyester, but only for a small percentage of their products, giving the impression that their entire brand is sustainable.

The consequences of greenwashing are far-reaching. It misleads consumers into believing that they are making sustainable choices, when in fact, their purchases may be contributing to environmental harm. This can undermine genuine efforts towards sustainability and create cynicism among consumers who feel betrayed by brands they trusted. Additionally, greenwashing can give unsustainable brands an unfair advantage over ethical brands that are genuinely committed to sustainability, hindering their growth and market share.

Identifying greenwashing requires a critical eye and a willingness to dig deeper than surface-level marketing claims. Here are some tips for spotting greenwashing:

Look for specific and verifiable claims: Vague claims like "eco-friendly" or "sustainable" should be backed up with concrete evidence, such as certifications from reputable organizations, detailed information about materials and production processes, and measurable goals for reducing environmental impact.

Be wary of buzzwords: Terms like "natural," "organic," and "biodegradable" can be misleading, as they don't necessarily guarantee sustainability. Look for specific details about how these terms are being used and what standards are being met.

Research the brand's overall practices: Don't just focus on individual products or claims. Look into the brand's overall commitment to sustainability, including their sourcing practices, labor standards, and environmental initiatives.

Check for third-party certifications: Look for certifications from reputable organizations that have rigorous standards and independent verification processes. These certifications can provide assurance that a brand is meeting certain environmental or social criteria.

Ask questions: If you're unsure about a brand's sustainability claims, don't hesitate to reach out to them and ask for more information. A truly sustainable brand will be transparent and willing to answer your questions.

As consumers, we have a responsibility to hold brands accountable for their sustainability claims. By demanding transparency and supporting ethical brands, we can create a market that rewards genuine sustainability efforts and discourages greenwashing. We can also use our voices to call out brands that engage in misleading practices and advocate for stronger regulations to protect consumers from greenwashing.

The fight against greenwashing is not just about protecting consumers; it's about ensuring that the fashion industry takes meaningful action towards sustainability. By identifying and rejecting greenwashing, we can create a market that incentivizes brands to invest in sustainable practices, leading to a more ethical and environmentally responsible fashion industry.

ᗡᗡᗡ

Your voice matters; use it to advocate for change. Fashion activism is about using your platform, no matter how small, to raise awareness and demand better from the industry. Be bold, be creative, and let your style speak volumes.

THIRTEEN

FASHION ACTIVISM: USING YOUR VOICE FOR CHANGE

Fashion activism is a dynamic and multifaceted movement that utilizes fashion as a powerful tool for social, political, and environmental change. It challenges the conventional notion of fashion as mere aesthetics and transforms it into a platform for activism, advocacy, and empowerment.

Fashion activism transcends the boundaries of the runway and enters the realms of social justice, environmental protection, and human rights, inspiring individuals and communities to use their voices and creativity to create a more sustainable and equitable world.

At its core, fashion activism is about using fashion as a medium to raise awareness, spark conversations, and challenge the status quo. It involves utilizing clothing, accessories, and personal style as a means of self-expression and a vehicle for social change.

Fashion activists use their creativity and platform to highlight pressing issues, challenge societal norms, and advocate for a more just and sustainable future.

Fashion activism takes many forms, from runway shows and fashion editorials that address social and environmental issues to social media campaigns and protests that mobilize communities and demand change.

It encompasses a wide range of voices and perspectives, from designers and models to consumers and activists, all united by a common goal of using fashion as a force for good.

One of the most powerful aspects of fashion activism is its ability to reach a wide audience and spark conversations about important issues. By using fashion as a medium, activists can tap into the cultural significance and emotional resonance of clothing, making their message more accessible and relatable to a broader audience.

This can lead to increased awareness and understanding of social and environmental issues, as well as inspire action and change.

Fashion activism has played a crucial role in raising awareness about the environmental impact of the fashion industry. From the devastating effects of fast fashion on natural resources and ecosystems to the exploitation of garment workers in developing countries, fashion activists have shed light on the dark side of the industry and advocated for more sustainable and ethical practices. They have called for greater transparency in supply chains, the use of eco-friendly materials, and fair labor practices.

In addition to environmental concerns, fashion activism has also been a powerful force for social justice. It has challenged traditional beauty standards, promoted inclusivity and diversity, and advocated for the rights of marginalized communities.

Fashion activists have used their platforms to speak out against racism, sexism, homophobia, and other forms of discrimination, using fashion as a tool for empowerment and self-expression.

The rise of social media has amplified the impact of fashion activism, allowing activists to connect with a global audience and mobilize communities around shared causes. Social media platforms, such as Instagram and Twitter, have become powerful tools for sharing information, organizing campaigns, and building solidarity among activists.

Hashtags like #WhoMadeMyClothes and #FashionRevolution have galvanized millions of people around the world to demand greater transparency and accountability from the fashion industry.

Fashion activism is not just about raising awareness and advocating for change; it is also about empowering individuals and communities to take action. By encouraging consumers to make more conscious and ethical choices about their clothing purchases, fashion activism can create a ripple effect that influences the entire industry.

It can also empower marginalized communities, such as garment workers and indigenous artisans, by providing them with a platform to share their stories and advocate for their rights.

However, fashion activism is not without its challenges. One of the main challenges is the risk of co-optation, where brands and businesses appropriate the language and imagery of activism without implementing meaningful change. This can dilute the message of activism and create cynicism among consumers who feel betrayed by brands they trusted.

Another challenge is the need for intersectionality. Fashion activism must address a wide range of issues, from environmental sustainability to social justice, and it must recognize the interconnectedness of these issues.

For example, the exploitation of garment workers is not just a labor rights issue; it is also an environmental issue, as it contributes to the overproduction and waste of clothing.

Despite these challenges, the future of fashion activism is bright. The movement is growing in strength and influence, as more and more people recognize the power of fashion to drive change. By using their voices and creativity, fashion activists are shaping a more sustainable, equitable, and just future for the fashion industry and the world.

ᗺᗺᗺ

*Sustainable style icons are not just trendsetters;
they are changemakers. Learn from their example,
be inspired by their choices, and use their influence
to create a more sustainable and equitable fashion
landscape. Together, we can make a difference.*

FOURTEEN

SUSTAINABLE STYLE ICONS: INSPIRATION FOR ETHICAL FASHION

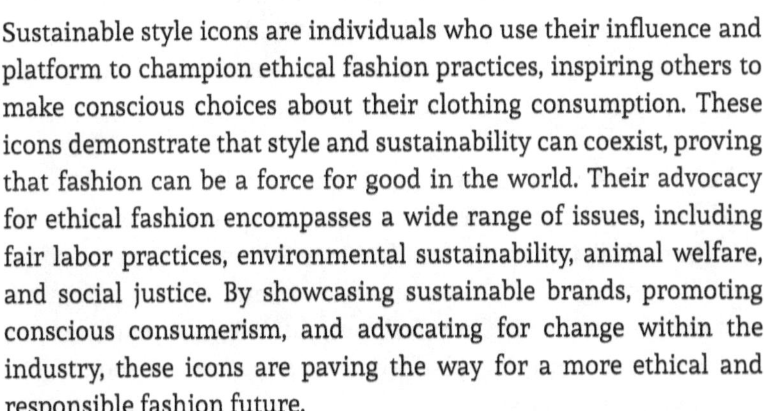

Sustainable style icons are individuals who use their influence and platform to champion ethical fashion practices, inspiring others to make conscious choices about their clothing consumption. These icons demonstrate that style and sustainability can coexist, proving that fashion can be a force for good in the world. Their advocacy for ethical fashion encompasses a wide range of issues, including fair labor practices, environmental sustainability, animal welfare, and social justice. By showcasing sustainable brands, promoting conscious consumerism, and advocating for change within the industry, these icons are paving the way for a more ethical and responsible fashion future.

One of the most prominent sustainable style icons is Stella McCartney, a British fashion designer who has been a pioneer in sustainable fashion since the inception of her eponymous brand in 2001. McCartney is known for her cruelty-free ethos, refusing to use leather, fur, or feathers in her designs. She has also been a vocal advocate for sustainable materials, such as organic cotton, recycled polyester, and regenerated cashmere. McCartney's commitment to sustainability has not only earned her critical acclaim but has also inspired other designers and brands to follow in her footsteps.

Another notable sustainable style icon is Emma Watson, an actress and activist who has used her platform to promote ethical fashion. Watson has collaborated with sustainable brands, such as People Tree and Good On You, and has been a vocal advocate for transparency and fair labor practices in the fashion industry. She has also used her social media presence to educate consumers about sustainable fashion and encourage them to make more conscious choices.

Livia Firth, the founder of Eco-Age, a sustainability consultancy firm, is another influential figure in the sustainable fashion movement. Firth has been instrumental in promoting the Green Carpet Challenge, an initiative that encourages celebrities to wear sustainable fashion on the red carpet. She has also worked with numerous brands and designers to help them incorporate sustainable practices into their businesses.

Other notable sustainable style icons include Arizona Muse, a model and environmental activist who has spoken out against the environmental impact of fast fashion; Summer Rayne Oakes, a model, author, and environmental scientist who promotes sustainable living and ethical fashion; and Wilson Oryema, a model and activist who uses his platform to raise awareness about social and environmental issues.

These are just a few examples of the many individuals who are using their influence to promote sustainable fashion. Their advocacy takes many forms, from social media campaigns and collaborations with ethical brands to speaking engagements and participation in industry events. By sharing their knowledge, experiences, and passion for sustainable fashion, these icons are inspiring a new generation of consumers to make more conscious choices and demand more from the fashion industry.

The impact of sustainable style icons is undeniable. Their advocacy has helped to raise awareness about the environmental and social impact of fast fashion, leading to increased demand for sustainable and ethical clothing. Their collaborations with brands have helped to bring sustainable fashion into the mainstream, making it more accessible and appealing to a wider audience. And their voices have helped to push the industry towards greater transparency, accountability, and sustainability.

The rise of sustainable style icons is a reflection of a growing cultural shift towards conscious consumerism. As consumers become more aware of the negative impacts of their consumption habits, they are increasingly seeking out brands and products that align with their values. This shift is particularly evident in the fashion industry, where the environmental and social costs of fast fashion are becoming increasingly apparent.

Sustainable style icons are playing a crucial role in this cultural shift by providing consumers with inspiration and guidance. They are showcasing the beauty and versatility of sustainable fashion, proving that ethical clothing can be both stylish and affordable. They are also educating consumers about the importance of sustainability, empowering them to make informed choices about their clothing purchases.

However, the work of sustainable style icons is not without its challenges. The fashion industry is deeply entrenched in unsustainable practices, and change can be slow and difficult. Additionally, greenwashing, the practice of making misleading or unsubstantiated claims about the environmental benefits of products, is a pervasive issue that can make it difficult for consumers to identify truly sustainable brands.

Despite these challenges, the future of sustainable fashion is bright. The growing influence of sustainable style icons, coupled with increasing consumer demand for ethical and sustainable clothing, is creating a powerful force for change within the industry. By continuing to raise awareness, promote sustainable practices, and inspire action, these icons are paving the way for a more ethical, equitable, and sustainable fashion future.

ᗡᗡᗡ

Caring for your clothes is an act of love for both your wardrobe and the planet. Mend, repair, and cherish your garments, extending their lifespan and reducing waste. Let your clothes tell a story of care, longevity, and timeless style.

FIFTEEN

WARDROBE CARE: EXTENDING THE LIFE OF YOUR CLOTHES

Wardrobe care is an often overlooked yet essential aspect of sustainable fashion. By adopting simple yet effective practices, we can significantly extend the lifespan of our clothes, reducing waste and minimizing our environmental impact. Caring for our clothes not only benefits the planet but also saves us money in the long run and allows us to cherish our favorite garments for years to come.

One of the most fundamental aspects of wardrobe care is proper washing. Many garments can be washed less frequently than we think. Overwashing can lead to fading, shrinkage, and overall wear and tear. Instead, consider airing out clothes after wearing them, spot cleaning stains, and washing them only when necessary.

When washing is required, follow the care instructions on the garment label and use a gentle detergent. Washing clothes in cold water can also help to conserve energy and prevent colors from fading.

Drying clothes properly is equally important. Air drying is the most eco-friendly and gentle option, as it avoids the high heat and tumbling of a dryer, which can damage fibers and cause shrinkage. If using a dryer is unavoidable, choose the lowest heat setting and remove clothes promptly to prevent wrinkles. For delicate items, lay them flat to dry to maintain their shape.

Storing clothes properly can also significantly impact their longevity. Avoid hanging heavy sweaters, as they can stretch and lose their shape. Instead, fold them and store them on shelves. Use padded hangers for delicate items like silk blouses or suits to prevent shoulder bumps and stretching.

Keep clothes in a cool, dry, and dark place to prevent fading and damage from sunlight. Cedar blocks or lavender sachets can help to repel moths and keep clothes smelling fresh.

Regular maintenance is another crucial aspect of wardrobe care. Mending small holes, tears, or loose buttons can prevent further damage and extend the life of a garment.

If you're not confident in your sewing skills, seek the help of a tailor or repair specialist. Investing in quality repairs can be far more cost-effective than replacing a garment altogether.

Rotating your wardrobe can also help to extend the life of your clothes. By wearing different items regularly, you can avoid overusing any single garment and prevent it from wearing out prematurely. This also allows your clothes to rest and recover between wears, which can help to maintain their shape and prevent wrinkles.

Proper footwear care is also important for extending the life of your shoes. This includes cleaning them regularly, storing them properly, and using shoe trees to maintain their shape. Leather shoes should be conditioned regularly to keep them supple and prevent cracking.

Suede shoes require special care, such as using a suede brush and protector spray. By taking care of your shoes, you can ensure that they last for years and avoid the need for frequent replacements.

Choosing quality garments is another key factor in extending the life of your clothes. Invest in well-made pieces from reputable brands that use durable materials and construction techniques. While high-quality garments may have a higher upfront cost, they will ultimately save you money in the long run as they will last longer and require less frequent replacement.

Consider the versatility of a garment before purchasing it. Choose pieces that can be easily mixed and matched with other items in your wardrobe, allowing you to create a variety of outfits. This not only maximizes the use of each garment but also reduces the need to buy new clothes for every occasion.

Taking care of your clothes is a conscious and responsible choice that benefits both the environment and your wallet. By adopting simple practices such as proper washing, drying, and storing, as well as regular maintenance and rotation, you can significantly extend the lifespan of your garments.

Choosing quality pieces and considering their versatility can further enhance the longevity of your wardrobe. By embracing wardrobe care, you are not only contributing to a more sustainable fashion industry but also creating a more personal and meaningful relationship with your clothes.

Wardrobe care is an ongoing process that requires commitment and attention to detail. However, the rewards are immeasurable. By taking care of your clothes, you are not only reducing waste and conserving resources but also preserving memories, stories, and emotions associated with each garment.

In a world of fast fashion and disposable consumerism, wardrobe care is a radical act of resistance, a celebration of craftsmanship, and a testament to the enduring power of personal style.

ϷϷϷ

Minimalism is not about sacrificing style; it's about embracing simplicity and functionality. Let your wardrobe reflect your values, not the latest trends. Choose quality over quantity and focus on timeless pieces that make you feel confident and comfortable.

SIXTEEN

Minimalist Fashion: Embracing Simplicity and Functionality

Minimalist fashion, a movement rooted in simplicity, functionality, and timeless elegance, has emerged as a powerful antidote to the excesses and fleeting trends of fast fashion. It is a philosophy that celebrates the beauty of clean lines, understated silhouettes, and a curated wardrobe of essential pieces. Minimalist fashion is not just a style; it's a lifestyle choice that prioritizes quality over quantity, mindful consumption over impulsive buying, and personal expression over conforming to trends.

At its core, minimalist fashion is about stripping away the unnecessary and focusing on the essentials. It's about curating a wardrobe of high-quality, versatile pieces that can be mixed and matched to create a variety of looks. It's about investing in timeless designs that transcend trends and stand the test of time. It's about embracing a less-is-more approach to fashion, where each piece is carefully chosen and cherished.

The minimalist aesthetic is characterized by clean lines, simple shapes, and a neutral color palette. It eschews excessive embellishments, logos, and patterns, opting instead for understated elegance and refined details. The focus is on the quality of the fabric, the cut of the garment, and the way it drapes on the body. Minimalist fashion celebrates the natural beauty of the wearer, allowing their personality and style to shine through.

Minimalist fashion is not just about aesthetics; it's also about functionality and practicality. Each piece in a minimalist wardrobe serves a purpose and is chosen for its versatility and ability to be worn in multiple ways. This approach not only simplifies dressing but also reduces the need for a large and overflowing wardrobe. It also encourages creativity and resourcefulness, as individuals learn to maximize the potential of each garment through different combinations and styling techniques.

The minimalist lifestyle extends beyond the wardrobe. It's about simplifying all aspects of life, from decluttering our homes and possessions to prioritizing experiences over material goods. It's about living intentionally and mindfully, focusing on what truly matters and letting go of excess. Minimalist fashion is a reflection of this philosophy, as it encourages us to be more conscious of our consumption habits and to prioritize quality and longevity over quantity and disposability.

Embracing minimalist fashion can have a profound impact on our lives. It can free us from the pressure to constantly consume new clothes and keep up with the latest trends. It can simplify our morning routines and reduce decision fatigue, as we have fewer choices but more confidence in our outfits. It can also save us money in the long run, as we invest in quality pieces that last longer and require less frequent replacement.

Minimalist fashion is also a more sustainable and ethical choice. By choosing quality over quantity, we reduce the demand for fast fashion, which is a major contributor to environmental pollution and waste. We also support brands that prioritize fair labor practices and use sustainable materials, contributing to a more ethical and responsible fashion industry.

Minimalist fashion is not a one-size-fits-all approach. It's about finding what works for you and your lifestyle. It's about creating a wardrobe that reflects your personal style and makes you feel confident and comfortable. It's about embracing simplicity, functionality, and timeless elegance in a way that feels authentic and empowering.

The benefits of minimalist fashion extend beyond personal style and sustainability. It can also have a positive impact on our mental and emotional well-being. By simplifying our lives and focusing on what truly matters, we can reduce stress and anxiety and cultivate a greater sense of contentment and peace. Minimalist fashion can also be a form of self-care, as it encourages us to prioritize comfort and functionality in our clothing choices.

While minimalist fashion may seem daunting at first, it can be a liberating and transformative experience. By decluttering our wardrobes, investing in quality pieces, and embracing simplicity, we can create a wardrobe that not only makes us look and feel good but also aligns with our values and contributes to a more sustainable and equitable world.

ᐅᐅᐅ

Sustainable accessories are the perfect complement to a conscious wardrobe. Choose shoes and bags made from eco-friendly materials and produced ethically. Let your accessories speak to your commitment to a sustainable future.

SEVENTEEN

SUSTAINABLE ACCESSORIES: ETHICAL CHOICES FOR SHOES AND BAGS

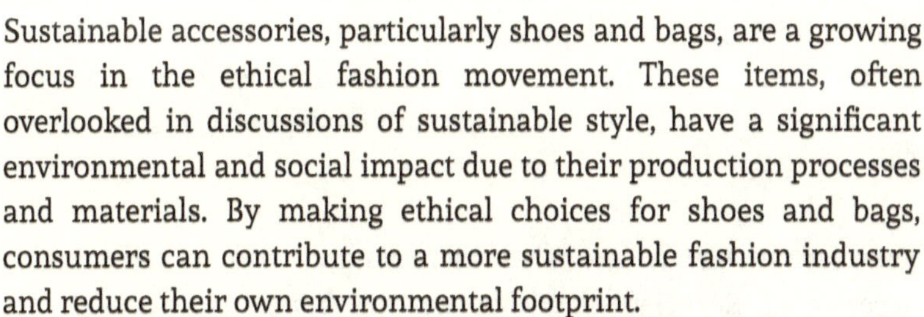

Sustainable accessories, particularly shoes and bags, are a growing focus in the ethical fashion movement. These items, often overlooked in discussions of sustainable style, have a significant environmental and social impact due to their production processes and materials. By making ethical choices for shoes and bags, consumers can contribute to a more sustainable fashion industry and reduce their own environmental footprint.

The production of shoes and bags often involves the use of resource-intensive materials, such as leather, synthetic fabrics, and metals. Leather production, for instance, is associated with deforestation, water pollution, and greenhouse gas emissions. Synthetic fabrics, often derived from petroleum, contribute to plastic pollution and can take centuries to decompose. The mining and processing of metals used in hardware and embellishments also have significant environmental consequences.

In addition to the environmental impact, the production of shoes and bags often involves ethical concerns. Many factories in developing countries, where a large portion of footwear and handbags are produced, have poor working conditions, low wages, and lack of labor rights protection. Child labor and forced labor are also prevalent in some supply chains.

Therefore, choosing sustainable accessories involves considering both the environmental and social impact of their production. This means opting for brands that prioritize transparency, fair labor practices, and sustainable materials. It also means being mindful of our consumption habits, investing in quality items that will last, and repairing or upcycling them when possible.

When it comes to sustainable materials, several options are gaining traction in the footwear and handbag industry. One such material is Piñatex, a leather alternative made from pineapple leaf fibers. It is a vegan and sustainable option that requires less water and land than traditional leather production. Another innovative material is mycelium, the root structure of mushrooms, which can be used to create leather-like materials that are biodegradable and cruelty-free.

Recycled materials are also increasingly used in sustainable accessories. Recycled plastic bottles are being transformed into durable fabrics for bags and shoes, while recycled rubber is used for soles. Some brands are even experimenting with recycled fishing nets and other ocean waste to create innovative and sustainable materials.

Ethical production practices are equally important in sustainable accessories. Fair trade certifications ensure that workers are paid fair wages and work in safe conditions. Look for brands that are transparent about their supply chains and have certifications from reputable organizations, such as Fairtrade International or the World Fair Trade Organization.

Choosing sustainable accessories also means being mindful of our consumption habits. Invest in quality items that are made to last, rather than buying cheap, disposable items that will quickly end up in landfills. Consider buying secondhand or vintage accessories, which can be a great way to find unique and stylish pieces while reducing waste.

Repairing and upcycling are also important aspects of sustainable accessory use. Instead of discarding damaged items, consider repairing them or finding creative ways to upcycle them into new accessories. This not only extends the lifespan of your items but also adds a personal touch to your style.

When shopping for sustainable shoes, consider brands that prioritize natural and recycled materials. Look for shoes made from organic cotton, hemp, or linen for uppers, and recycled rubber or natural cork for soles. Some brands also use innovative materials like algae-based foam for cushioning and recycled ocean plastic for laces.

For bags, consider options made from organic cotton, hemp, or recycled materials. Look for bags with minimal hardware and embellishments, as these can be difficult to recycle. Also, consider the size and functionality of the bag. A versatile bag that can be used for multiple purposes can reduce the need to buy multiple bags for different occasions.

Sustainable accessories are not just about eco-friendly materials and ethical production; they are also about style and functionality.

Many sustainable brands offer stylish and trendy designs that rival conventional brands. From minimalist leather sneakers to colorful recycled tote bags, there are plenty of options to suit different tastes and needs.

By choosing sustainable accessories, consumers can make a positive impact on the environment and the lives of the people who make their clothes. They can also express their personal style while contributing to a more sustainable and ethical fashion industry.

❦❦❦

Sustainable beauty is about nourishing your skin and the planet. Choose products made with natural, organic, and cruelty-free ingredients. Let your beauty routine reflect your love for yourself and the environment.

EIGHTEEN

SUSTAINABLE BEAUTY: ECO-FRIENDLY MAKEUP AND SKINCARE

Sustainable beauty is a growing movement within the beauty industry that prioritizes eco-friendly practices, ethical sourcing, and non-toxic ingredients. It encompasses a wide range of products, from makeup and skincare to haircare and personal care items. By embracing sustainable beauty, consumers can not only enhance their natural beauty but also contribute to a healthier planet and support brands that prioritize social and environmental responsibility.

The traditional beauty industry has long been criticized for its environmental impact. From excessive packaging waste to the use of harmful chemicals and unsustainable sourcing practices, the production and consumption of beauty products have taken a toll on the environment. However, the rise of sustainable beauty brands is challenging this status quo, offering consumers a more conscious and eco-friendly alternative.

One of the key aspects of sustainable beauty is the use of eco-friendly packaging. Sustainable beauty brands are increasingly moving away from single-use plastics and opting for recyclable, reusable, or biodegradable packaging materials. This not only reduces waste but also minimizes the environmental impact of the beauty industry.

Another important aspect of sustainable beauty is the use of natural and organic ingredients. These ingredients are grown without the use of harmful pesticides and fertilizers, making them safer for both the environment and human health. Many sustainable beauty brands also prioritize ethical sourcing, ensuring that their ingredients are harvested in a way that supports local communities and protects biodiversity.

Sustainable beauty brands also strive to minimize their water and energy consumption during production. They often invest in renewable energy sources, such as solar and wind power, and implement water-saving technologies to reduce their environmental footprint.

Beyond environmental concerns, sustainable beauty also addresses social and ethical issues. Many sustainable beauty brands are committed to fair trade practices, ensuring that their workers are paid fair wages and work in safe and healthy conditions. They also support social initiatives that empower women and promote sustainable development in their communities.

The benefits of sustainable beauty are numerous. By choosing eco-friendly makeup and skincare products, consumers can reduce their exposure to harmful chemicals and toxins. These chemicals, often found in conventional beauty products, can disrupt hormones, irritate skin, and even contribute to chronic diseases. Sustainable beauty products, on the other hand, are often formulated with natural and organic ingredients that are gentle on the skin and promote overall health and well-being.

Sustainable beauty also benefits the environment. By choosing products with eco-friendly packaging and sustainably sourced ingredients, consumers can reduce their environmental footprint and support brands that are committed to protecting the planet. Additionally, sustainable beauty brands often prioritize cruelty-free practices, refusing to test their products on animals.

Choosing sustainable beauty products does not mean sacrificing quality or effectiveness. Many sustainable beauty brands offer high-performance products that are just as effective, if not more so, than their conventional counterparts. With advancements in green chemistry and the use of innovative natural ingredients, sustainable beauty brands are creating products that deliver results without compromising on sustainability.

However, navigating the world of sustainable beauty can be challenging. Greenwashing, the practice of making misleading or unsubstantiated claims about the environmental benefits of products, is a pervasive issue in the beauty industry. It can be difficult for consumers to distinguish between truly sustainable brands and those that are simply using green marketing tactics to appeal to environmentally conscious consumers.

To make informed choices, consumers can look for certifications from reputable organizations, such as Ecocert, COSMOS, and B Corp. These certifications indicate that a brand meets rigorous standards for environmental and social responsibility. Additionally, consumers can research brands online, read reviews, and look for transparency in their ingredient sourcing and production processes.

The sustainable beauty movement is gaining momentum as more and more consumers become aware of the impact of their beauty choices. By choosing eco-friendly makeup and skincare products, supporting ethical brands, and advocating for greater transparency and sustainability within the industry, we can create a beauty industry that is not only good for us but also for the planet.

ppp

Fashion rental is a revolutionary concept that challenges the traditional model of ownership. Embrace the freedom of access over possession, experiment with different styles, and reduce your environmental footprint.

NINETEEN

FASHION RENTAL: A SUSTAINABLE ALTERNATIVE TO OWNERSHIP

Fashion rental has emerged as a revolutionary concept in the fashion industry, offering a sustainable alternative to the traditional model of clothing ownership. This innovative approach allows individuals to access a wide variety of garments and accessories for a limited period, typically a few days or weeks, without the need to purchase them outright. By shifting the focus from ownership to access, fashion rental addresses the environmental and social issues associated with fast fashion, promotes a more circular economy, and empowers consumers to embrace a more sustainable and diverse wardrobe.

The traditional model of clothing ownership, characterized by the constant purchase of new garments to keep up with trends, has led to a culture of overconsumption and disposability. The fast fashion industry, with its rapid production cycles and low-quality garments, has exacerbated this issue, contributing to a massive accumulation of textile waste and environmental pollution. Fashion rental offers a compelling solution to this problem by decoupling consumption from ownership and promoting the reuse and sharing of garments.

One of the primary benefits of fashion rental is its potential to reduce the environmental impact of the fashion industry. By renting clothes instead of buying them, consumers can significantly reduce their carbon footprint and water usage. The production of new clothing requires vast amounts of resources, including water, energy, and chemicals, and contributes to greenhouse gas emissions and pollution. By extending the lifespan of garments through rental, we can minimize the demand for new clothing production and reduce the associated environmental impact.

Fashion rental also promotes a more circular economy by keeping garments in circulation for longer periods. Instead of being discarded after a few wears, rented garments are returned to the rental company, where they are cleaned, repaired, and rented out again. This not only reduces waste but also creates a more sustainable and efficient use of resources.

Another significant advantage of fashion rental is its potential to democratize fashion and make high-end designer clothing accessible to a wider audience. Renting allows individuals to experiment with different styles, brands, and trends without the financial commitment of purchasing them outright. This is particularly appealing to younger generations who are increasingly prioritizing experiences over material possessions.

Furthermore, fashion rental can help to reduce the social impact of the fashion industry. By extending the lifespan of garments, rental platforms can create more sustainable and stable jobs for workers in the garment industry. Additionally, many rental companies are committed to ethical sourcing and fair labor practices, ensuring that the people who make our clothes are treated fairly and paid a living wage.

The rise of fashion rental has been facilitated by the growth of online platforms and technological advancements. These platforms offer a wide range of rental options, from everyday wear to special occasion dresses and accessories. They also provide convenient services, such as online browsing, home delivery, and professional cleaning. This has made fashion rental more accessible and appealing to consumers, particularly those who are tech-savvy and environmentally conscious.

However, fashion rental is not without its challenges. One of the main concerns is the hygiene of rented garments. While rental companies typically have strict cleaning protocols in place, some consumers may still be hesitant to wear clothes that have been worn by others. Another challenge is the potential for damage to rented garments. Rental companies often have policies in place to address this issue, but it can still be a deterrent for some consumers.

Despite these challenges, the future of fashion rental looks bright. As consumers become more aware of the environmental and social impact of their clothing choices, the demand for sustainable alternatives like fashion rental is expected to grow. Additionally, technological advancements, such as blockchain technology, are being explored to improve the traceability and transparency of rental garments, further enhancing consumer confidence.

Fashion rental is not just a trend; it is a paradigm shift in the way we consume fashion. By embracing this sustainable alternative to ownership, we can reduce our environmental footprint, promote a circular economy, democratize fashion, and create a more ethical and responsible fashion industry.

ppp

Your wedding day should be a celebration of love and sustainability. Choose eco-friendly bridal fashion that reflects your values and minimizes your impact on the planet. Let your dress be a symbol of your commitment to a beautiful and sustainable future.

TWENTY

SUSTAINABLE WEDDINGS: ECO-FRIENDLY BRIDAL FASHION

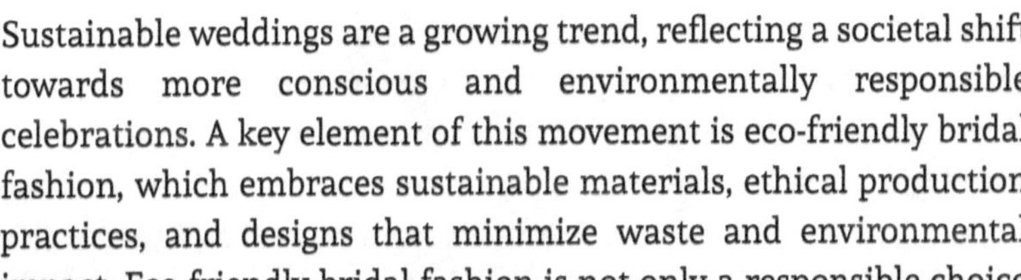

Sustainable weddings are a growing trend, reflecting a societal shift towards more conscious and environmentally responsible celebrations. A key element of this movement is eco-friendly bridal fashion, which embraces sustainable materials, ethical production practices, and designs that minimize waste and environmental impact. Eco-friendly bridal fashion is not only a responsible choice for the planet but also allows brides to express their personal style while aligning their values with their special day.

Traditional bridal fashion has often been associated with extravagance, excess, and a disregard for environmental concerns. Wedding dresses are often made from resource-intensive materials, such as silk and synthetic fabrics, and are frequently worn only once before being discarded. This disposable culture contributes to textile waste, pollution, and the exploitation of natural resources. However, eco-friendly bridal fashion offers a refreshing alternative, proving that bridal wear can be both beautiful and sustainable.

One of the cornerstones of eco-friendly bridal fashion is the use of sustainable materials. This involves choosing fabrics that have a lower environmental impact than conventional materials, such as organic cotton, hemp, linen, bamboo, and recycled fibers. These materials are often grown or produced using less water, energy, and chemicals than their conventional counterparts, and they may also be biodegradable or recyclable at the end of their life.

Organic cotton, for example, is grown without the use of harmful pesticides and fertilizers, making it a safer and more sustainable option for both the environment and the farmers who grow it. Hemp, a versatile fiber known for its strength and durability, requires minimal water and pesticides to grow, making it a responsible choice for a variety of bridal wear applications. Linen, derived from the flax plant, is another sustainable option that is known for its breathability and natural elegance.

Recycled fabrics, made from post-consumer or post-industrial waste, are also gaining popularity in eco-friendly bridal fashion. These fabrics offer a way to reduce waste and minimize the demand for virgin materials. Recycled polyester, for example, is made from plastic bottles and can be used to create beautiful and durable wedding dresses. Recycled lace, made from vintage or reclaimed lace, adds a touch of romance and history to bridal wear.

In addition to sustainable materials, eco-friendly bridal fashion also embraces ethical production practices. This means ensuring that the people who make our wedding dresses are treated fairly and paid a living wage. It also means ensuring that the production process minimizes waste and pollution and adheres to sustainable practices.

Many eco-conscious brides are choosing to support fair trade fashion brands that prioritize social and environmental responsibility. These brands often partner with artisans and cooperatives in developing countries, providing them with fair wages and safe working conditions. By choosing fair trade bridal wear, brides can contribute to the empowerment of women and the economic development of communities.

Another way to embrace eco-friendly bridal fashion is to opt for vintage or secondhand wedding dresses. This not only reduces waste but also adds a unique and personal touch to the wedding day. Vintage dresses often have a timeless elegance and charm that cannot be replicated by modern designs. Additionally, they often offer a more affordable option for brides on a budget.

Renting a wedding dress is another sustainable alternative that is gaining popularity. Several online platforms and brick-and-mortar stores now offer wedding dress rentals, allowing brides to wear designer gowns for a fraction of the cost of buying them. This option not only reduces waste but also allows brides to experiment with different styles and designers without the commitment of ownership.

Designing a wedding dress that can be worn again after the wedding is another way to embrace eco-friendly bridal fashion. Some brides are opting for convertible dresses that can be transformed into different styles for future events. Others are choosing simple and versatile designs that can be easily dressed up or down for different occasions.

The sustainable wedding movement is not just about the bride's attire. It also encompasses other aspects of the wedding, such as the choice of venue, decorations, food, and favors. By making conscious choices throughout the wedding planning process, couples can create a celebration that is not only beautiful and memorable but also environmentally responsible.

Sustainable weddings are a testament to the growing awareness of the importance of environmental sustainability and social responsibility. By embracing eco-friendly bridal fashion and other sustainable practices, couples can create a wedding that reflects their values and contributes to a healthier planet. It's a celebration of love that also honors the Earth and its resources.

❦❦❦

Sustainable menswear is not just a trend; it's a movement towards a more ethical and eco-conscious approach to fashion. Choose timeless pieces made from sustainable materials and support brands that prioritize fair labor practices.

TWENTY-ONE

SUSTAINABLE MENSWEAR: ETHICAL FASHION FOR MEN

Sustainable menswear is a growing movement that seeks to redefine the way men dress, by prioritizing ethical production, environmental responsibility, and conscious consumption. It challenges the traditional norms of the fashion industry, which have often prioritized profit and trends over sustainability and social impact. Sustainable menswear offers an alternative path, one that allows men to express their style while also contributing to a more ethical and eco-conscious future.

The rise of fast fashion has had a detrimental impact on the environment and society. The rapid production cycles, cheap materials, and disposable nature of fast fashion garments have led to a massive accumulation of textile waste, pollution, and the exploitation of workers. The menswear industry, while often overshadowed by the women's wear market, is not immune to these issues.

Sustainable menswear aims to address these problems by embracing a more holistic approach to fashion. It considers the entire lifecycle of a garment, from the sourcing of raw materials and the manufacturing process to the end-of-life disposal. It also emphasizes quality over quantity, encouraging men to invest in timeless pieces that are made to last.

One of the key aspects of sustainable menswear is the use of eco-friendly materials. This involves choosing fabrics that have a lower environmental impact than conventional materials, such as organic cotton, hemp, linen, bamboo, and recycled fibers. These materials are often grown or produced using less water, energy, and chemicals than their conventional counterparts, and they may also be biodegradable or recyclable at the end of their life.

Organic cotton, for example, is grown without the use of harmful pesticides and fertilizers, making it a safer and more sustainable option for both the environment and the farmers who grow it. Hemp, a versatile fiber known for its strength and durability, requires minimal water and pesticides to grow, making it an ideal choice for various menswear items. Linen, derived from the flax plant, is another sustainable option that is known for its breathability and natural elegance.

Recycled fabrics, made from post-consumer or post-industrial waste, are also gaining popularity in sustainable menswear. These fabrics offer a way to reduce waste and minimize the demand for virgin materials. Recycled polyester, for example, is made from plastic bottles and can be used to create durable and stylish menswear items.

Another crucial aspect of sustainable menswear is ethical production. This involves ensuring that the people who make our clothes are treated fairly and paid a living wage. It also means ensuring that the manufacturing process minimizes environmental impact and adheres to social responsibility standards.

Many sustainable menswear brands are committed to fair trade practices, partnering with factories and suppliers that uphold ethical labor standards. They also prioritize transparency in their supply chains, allowing consumers to trace the origin of their garments and verify that they were produced under safe and fair conditions.

Slow fashion is another key principle of sustainable menswear. This movement encourages consumers to buy less clothing, but of higher quality, that will last longer. It also emphasizes timeless styles and classic designs that are not dictated by fleeting trends, thus reducing the need to constantly update one's wardrobe.

By investing in quality pieces that are made to last, men can not only reduce their environmental impact but also save money in the long run. Sustainable menswear brands often use high-quality materials and construction techniques, resulting in garments that are durable, long-lasting, and less likely to need frequent replacement.

Sustainable menswear is not just about buying new clothes; it's also about caring for the clothes you already own. This means washing them less frequently, using gentle detergents, and air-drying them whenever possible. It also means repairing damaged garments instead of discarding them and donating unwanted clothes to charity or recycling programs.

The rise of sustainable menswear is a reflection of a growing awareness among men of the importance of sustainability and ethical consumerism. It's a recognition that our clothing choices have a significant impact on the environment and the people who make our clothes. By choosing sustainable menswear, men can express their style while also contributing to a more sustainable and equitable future.

In addition to environmental and social benefits, sustainable menswear can also be a source of personal satisfaction and empowerment. By making conscious choices about the clothes we wear, we can align our values with our actions and feel good about the impact we are having on the world. We can also discover new brands and designers that are creating innovative and stylish sustainable menswear, challenging the notion that ethical fashion is boring or unattractive.

The future of menswear is sustainable. As the demand for ethical and eco-conscious clothing grows, more and more brands are incorporating sustainable practices into their business models. This is a positive development for the industry and the planet, and it offers men the opportunity to dress well while also making a difference.

ᐅᐅᐅ

Sustainable activewear allows you to pursue your fitness goals while minimizing your environmental impact. Choose workout clothes made from recycled or natural materials and support brands that prioritize ethical production.

TWENTY-TWO

SUSTAINABLE ACTIVEWEAR: ECO-FRIENDLY WORKOUT CLOTHES

Sustainable activewear is revolutionizing the athletic apparel industry by offering eco-friendly workout clothes that prioritize environmental responsibility and ethical production. As consumers become increasingly aware of the environmental and social impact of their clothing choices, the demand for sustainable activewear has surged, driving innovation and change within the industry. This movement towards eco-conscious workout gear not only benefits the planet but also provides athletes and fitness enthusiasts with high-performance clothing that aligns with their values.

The traditional activewear industry has long relied on synthetic fabrics derived from petroleum, such as polyester and nylon. While these materials offer desirable performance properties, such as moisture-wicking and quick-drying capabilities, their production and disposal have significant environmental consequences. The extraction of fossil fuels for synthetic fibers contributes to greenhouse gas emissions and pollution, while the non-biodegradable nature of these materials leads to the accumulation of textile waste in landfills.

Sustainable activewear brands are challenging this status quo by seeking out alternative materials and production methods that minimize environmental impact. One of the most promising developments is the use of recycled materials. Recycled polyester, made from plastic bottles and other post-consumer waste, is a popular choice for sustainable activewear. It offers the same performance benefits as virgin polyester but with a significantly lower environmental footprint.

Natural fibers, such as organic cotton, bamboo, and hemp, are also gaining traction in the sustainable activewear market. These fibers are renewable, biodegradable, and often grown without the use of harmful pesticides and fertilizers. Organic cotton, for example, is a softer and more breathable alternative to conventional cotton, making it ideal for activewear. Bamboo fabric is known for its moisture-wicking and antibacterial properties, while hemp offers durability and natural UV protection.

In addition to using sustainable materials, eco-conscious activewear brands also prioritize ethical production practices. This means ensuring that workers are paid fair wages, work in safe and healthy conditions, and have the right to organize and bargain collectively. Many sustainable activewear brands also partner with factories and suppliers that adhere to strict environmental standards, minimizing waste, pollution, and energy consumption during production.

Transparency is another key aspect of sustainable activewear. Ethical brands are open and honest about their supply chains, allowing consumers to trace the origins of their garments and verify that they were produced responsibly. This transparency builds trust with consumers and empowers them to make informed choices about the brands they support.

The benefits of sustainable activewear are numerous. By choosing eco-friendly workout clothes, consumers can reduce their environmental footprint, conserve resources, and support ethical production practices. They can also enjoy the benefits of high-performance fabrics that are gentle on the skin and offer superior comfort and functionality.

Sustainable activewear is not just a trend; it is a movement towards a more responsible and conscious approach to athletic apparel. As consumers become more aware of the impact of their choices, the demand for sustainable activewear will continue to grow, driving innovation and change within the industry.

However, there are still challenges to overcome. One of the main challenges is the cost. Sustainable materials and ethical production practices can be more expensive than conventional methods, making sustainable activewear less accessible to some consumers. However, as the demand for sustainable products grows, the cost is expected to decrease, making them more accessible to a wider audience.

Another challenge is the durability of some sustainable materials. While natural fibers are often biodegradable and renewable, they may not be as durable as synthetic fibers, especially in high-intensity activities. However, advancements in textile technology are constantly improving the durability and performance of sustainable materials, making them a viable option for even the most demanding athletes.

Despite these challenges, the future of activewear is sustainable. As consumers demand more ethical and eco-conscious options, brands are responding by innovating and creating high-quality workout clothes that are both stylish and sustainable. This shift towards sustainability is not only good for the planet but also for the people who make and wear these clothes. By choosing sustainable activewear, we can all contribute to a healthier planet and a more ethical fashion industry.

ᗵᗵᗵ

Dress your children in sustainable kidswear that is gentle on their skin and the planet. Choose organic cotton, recycled fabrics, and other eco-friendly materials. Let your children's clothes be a reflection of your commitment to a sustainable future.

TWENTY-THREE

SUSTAINABLE KIDSWEAR: ETHICAL FASHION FOR CHILDREN

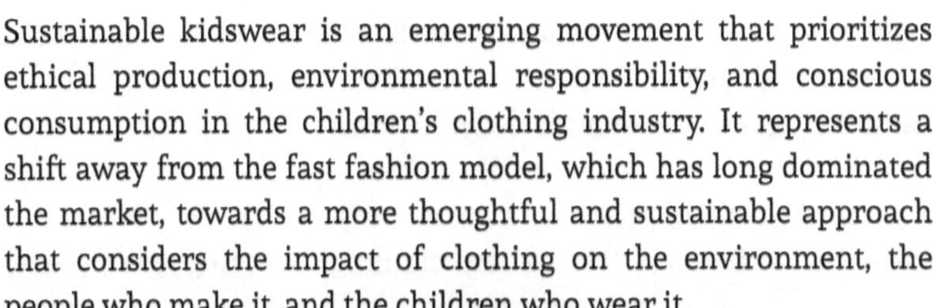

Sustainable kidswear is an emerging movement that prioritizes ethical production, environmental responsibility, and conscious consumption in the children's clothing industry. It represents a shift away from the fast fashion model, which has long dominated the market, towards a more thoughtful and sustainable approach that considers the impact of clothing on the environment, the people who make it, and the children who wear it.

The fast fashion industry has had a profound impact on the children's clothing market. With its emphasis on cheap, trendy clothes and rapid production cycles, fast fashion has made it easier than ever for parents to outfit their children in the latest styles. However, this convenience comes at a significant cost. Fast fashion is a major contributor to environmental pollution, waste, and the exploitation of workers, including children.

The production of children's clothing involves the use of large quantities of water, energy, and chemicals, and the disposal of unwanted clothes contributes to the growing problem of textile waste. Moreover, many fast fashion brands source their materials from countries with lax labor laws and environmental regulations, where workers, including children, are often paid low wages and forced to work in unsafe conditions.

Sustainable kidswear seeks to address these issues by prioritizing ethical production, environmental responsibility, and conscious consumption. Ethical production involves ensuring that the people who make children's clothes are treated fairly and paid a living wage. It also means ensuring that the manufacturing process minimizes environmental impact and adheres to social responsibility standards.

Environmental responsibility in the context of kidswear means using sustainable materials and production methods that minimize waste and pollution. This can involve using organic cotton, recycled fabrics, and other eco-friendly materials. It can also involve using water-saving technologies, renewable energy sources, and minimizing the use of harmful chemicals.

Conscious consumption is another key aspect of sustainable kidswear. It involves buying less clothing, choosing quality over quantity, and prioritizing durability and longevity. It also means taking care of clothes to extend their lifespan, repairing them when necessary, and passing them on to others when they are outgrown.

There are many reasons to choose sustainable kidswear. First and foremost, it's a more ethical and responsible choice. By supporting brands that prioritize fair labor practices and environmental sustainability, parents can help to create a more just and equitable fashion industry.

Sustainable kidswear is also a healthier choice for children. Many conventional children's clothes are made with harmful chemicals, such as flame retardants, formaldehyde, and heavy metals, which can irritate the skin and cause other health problems. Sustainable brands often avoid these chemicals, opting for natural and organic materials that are gentler on children's sensitive skin.

In addition to being ethical and healthy, sustainable kidswear can also be stylish and fun. Many sustainable brands offer a wide range of trendy and unique designs that appeal to children of all ages. These brands often prioritize comfort and functionality, creating clothes that are both stylish and practical for everyday wear.

Choosing sustainable kidswear is also an investment in the future. By teaching children about the importance of sustainability and ethical consumerism, we can help to create a more conscious and responsible generation of consumers. We can also show them that fashion can be a force for good, supporting communities and protecting the environment.

There are many ways to incorporate sustainable practices into your child's wardrobe. Start by choosing brands that prioritize ethical production and environmental responsibility. Look for certifications, such as GOTS (Global Organic Textile Standard) and Fairtrade, which indicate that a brand meets rigorous social and environmental standards.

Consider buying secondhand or vintage clothing. Not only is this a more sustainable option, but it can also be a fun and affordable way to find unique and stylish pieces for your child. You can also participate in clothing swaps with other parents or donate outgrown clothes to charity.

When buying new clothes, prioritize quality over quantity. Invest in well-made pieces that will last longer and can be passed down to siblings or friends. Choose versatile items that can be mixed and matched to create a variety of outfits, and avoid fast fashion trends that will quickly go out of style.

Teach your children about the importance of caring for their clothes. Encourage them to mend small holes or tears, and to wash their clothes less frequently and in cold water to conserve energy and extend their lifespan.

By making conscious choices about your child's clothing, you can not only reduce your environmental impact but also teach them valuable lessons about sustainability, ethics, and social responsibility. Sustainable kidswear is not just a trend; it's a movement towards a more responsible and conscious approach to fashion. By embracing this movement, we can create a better future for our children and the planet.

ᐅᐅᐅ

Sustainable travel is about exploring the world responsibly. Pack light and green, choose eco-friendly transportation and accommodations, and support local communities. Let your travels be a force for good.

TWENTY-FOUR

SUSTAINABLE TRAVEL: PACKING LIGHT AND GREEN

Sustainable travel, a burgeoning trend among conscious globetrotters, is transforming the way we explore the world. This approach to travel prioritizes minimizing environmental impact, supporting local communities, and making ethical choices throughout the journey.

A key aspect of sustainable travel is packing light and green, a practice that not only reduces your carbon footprint but also enhances your travel experience by simplifying logistics and allowing you to focus on the essence of your journey.

The concept of packing light and green involves several strategies that aim to minimize waste, conserve resources, and make responsible choices when it comes to what you bring on your travels. It entails packing only the essentials, choosing versatile and eco-friendly clothing and accessories, and being mindful of the impact of your choices on the environment and local communities.

One of the most effective ways to pack light and green is to create a capsule wardrobe for your trip. This involves selecting a limited number of versatile pieces that can be mixed and matched to create a variety of outfits suitable for different occasions and climates. By choosing timeless and classic styles, you can avoid overpacking and reduce the need to constantly buy new clothes during your travels.

When selecting clothes for your capsule wardrobe, prioritize quality over quantity. Invest in well-made garments from sustainable brands that use eco-friendly materials and ethical production practices. Look for clothes made from organic cotton, hemp, linen, or recycled fibers, as these materials have a lower environmental impact than conventional fabrics.

Opt for clothes that are durable and versatile, such as wrinkle-resistant shirts, quick-drying pants, and layering pieces that can be adapted to different temperatures.

Accessories can also play a crucial role in packing light and green. Choose versatile accessories that can be worn with multiple outfits, such as scarves, belts, and jewelry. Opt for multi-functional items, such as a sarong that can be used as a beach cover-up, a scarf, or a blanket. Consider packing a reusable water bottle and shopping bag to reduce waste and avoid single-use plastics.

Toiletries are another area where you can make sustainable choices. Instead of buying travel-sized toiletries that generate excess packaging waste, consider refilling reusable containers with your favorite products. Look for solid toiletries, such as shampoo bars and soap bars, which are not only more eco-friendly but also more convenient for travel as they eliminate the risk of spills and leaks.

Choosing eco-friendly luggage is another way to embrace sustainable travel. Look for luggage made from recycled materials or durable materials that will last for years. Consider investing in a lightweight suitcase or backpack to reduce the weight of your luggage and minimize fuel consumption during transportation.

When packing your luggage, use packing cubes or compression bags to maximize space and minimize wrinkles. Roll your clothes instead of folding them to save space and prevent creases. Avoid packing unnecessary items, such as bulky books or electronics that you can access digitally.

In addition to packing light and green, there are several other ways to make your travels more sustainable. Choose eco-friendly transportation options, such as trains or buses, whenever possible.

Support local businesses and communities by eating at local restaurants, staying in locally owned accommodations, and purchasing souvenirs from local artisans. Respect local customs and traditions, and be mindful of your impact on the environment and the local community.

Sustainable travel is not just about minimizing your environmental impact; it's also about enriching your travel experience. By packing light and green, you can simplify your logistics, reduce stress, and focus on the joys of exploring new places and cultures.

You can also connect with like-minded travelers and locals who share your values, creating a more meaningful and fulfilling travel experience.

The benefits of sustainable travel extend far beyond the individual traveler. By making conscious choices about our travel habits, we can contribute to a more sustainable and equitable tourism industry. We can support local communities, protect the environment, and create a positive impact on the places we visit.

As the world becomes more aware of the environmental and social consequences of our actions, the demand for sustainable travel options is growing.

More and more travelers are seeking out eco-friendly accommodations, transportation, and activities. The rise of sustainable travel is a testament to the power of individual action and the collective desire to create a more sustainable future for our planet.

ᐅᐅᐅ

The future of fashion lies in sustainability. Embrace ethical practices, circularity, and conscious consumption. Together, we can create a fashion industry that is not only stylish but also responsible, equitable, and regenerative.

TWENTY-FIVE

THE FUTURE OF FASHION: CREATING A SUSTAINABLE INDUSTRY

The future of fashion is inextricably linked to sustainability. The traditional model of fast fashion, characterized by rapid production cycles, cheap labor, and disposable garments, is no longer viable in a world grappling with climate change, resource depletion, and social inequality. The industry is at a crossroads, facing mounting pressure from consumers, activists, and policymakers to transform its practices and embrace a more sustainable future.

The concept of sustainable fashion encompasses a wide range of initiatives and approaches that aim to minimize the negative impact of the fashion industry on the environment and society. It involves a paradigm shift from a linear, take-make-dispose model to a circular model, where resources are kept in use for as long as possible, waste is minimized, and materials are recycled or reused. It also entails ethical sourcing and production practices, ensuring that workers are treated fairly and paid a living wage.

One of the key drivers of change in the fashion industry is consumer demand. As awareness of the environmental and social cost of fast fashion grows, consumers are increasingly seeking out sustainable alternatives. They are demanding transparency in supply chains, ethical sourcing practices, and eco-friendly materials. This shift in consumer behavior is forcing brands to rethink their practices and invest in sustainability initiatives.

Another driving force is technological innovation. New technologies, such as 3D printing, digital design, and blockchain, are being explored to create more efficient and sustainable production processes. 3D printing, for example, can reduce waste and minimize the need for transportation by allowing garments to be produced on demand, closer to the consumer. Digital design can help to streamline the design process, reducing the need for physical samples and minimizing waste. Blockchain technology can be used to track the origin of materials and ensure transparency in supply chains.

The rise of the sharing economy is also transforming the fashion industry. Clothing rental platforms, such as Rent the Runway and Le Tote, are offering consumers an alternative to ownership, allowing them to access a wider range of garments without the environmental and financial burden of buying them outright. This model not only reduces waste but also promotes a more circular economy, where garments are kept in circulation for longer periods.

The secondhand market is also booming, with online platforms like ThredUp and Depop providing a convenient and accessible way for consumers to buy and sell pre-loved clothing. This not only extends the lifespan of garments but also offers a more affordable and sustainable way to shop for fashion.

Policymakers are also playing a role in shaping the future of fashion. Several countries have introduced legislation aimed at promoting sustainability in the fashion industry. For example, France has banned the destruction of unsold clothing, requiring brands to donate or recycle unsold items. The European Union is also developing a strategy for sustainable textiles, which aims to promote circularity and reduce the environmental impact of textile production and consumption.

The future of fashion also lies in collaboration and partnerships. Brands, retailers, manufacturers, NGOs, and policymakers are increasingly working together to address the challenges facing the industry. Initiatives like the Fashion Pact, a global coalition of fashion companies committed to sustainability, are driving collective action to reduce the industry's environmental impact.

Education and awareness-raising are also crucial for creating a sustainable fashion industry. Consumers need to be informed about the environmental and social impact of their clothing choices, as well as the sustainable alternatives available. This can be achieved through educational campaigns, labeling initiatives, and collaborations between brands and NGOs.

The future of fashion is a complex and multifaceted issue, but one thing is clear: sustainability is no longer a niche concern but a fundamental requirement for the industry's survival and growth. By embracing sustainable materials, ethical production practices, circular business models, and consumer education, the fashion industry can transform itself into a force for good, one that not only produces beautiful clothes but also protects the planet and empowers its people.

The transition to a sustainable fashion industry will not be easy, but it is necessary. It requires a collective effort from all stakeholders, including brands, retailers, manufacturers, consumers, and policymakers. However, the potential benefits are immense. A sustainable fashion industry can not only reduce its environmental impact and improve social conditions but also create new economic opportunities, foster innovation, and inspire a new generation of consumers to embrace a more conscious and responsible approach to fashion.

ᐅᐅᐅ

Let your wardrobe be a reflection of your values, a testament to your commitment to a more sustainable and ethical world. Choose wisely, consume consciously, and let your style speak volumes about the change you want to see in the world.

TWENTY-SIX
SUMMARY

The journey through the world of sustainable fashion, as explored in the preceding chapters, reveals a complex tapestry woven with threads of environmental consciousness, ethical considerations, and personal style. This summary chapter aims to synthesize the key takeaways from this exploration, providing a comprehensive overview of the various facets of sustainable fashion and empowering readers to make informed choices that align with their values and contribute to a more responsible and equitable fashion industry.

The hidden cost of fast fashion, as revealed in Chapter 1, serves as a stark reminder of the environmental and social consequences of our insatiable appetite for cheap and trendy clothing. The industry's reliance on resource-intensive materials, exploitative labor practices, and wasteful production methods has a devastating impact on the planet and its people. However, the emergence of sustainable style, as defined in Chapter 2, offers a beacon of hope, showcasing a more ethical and eco-friendly approach to fashion that prioritizes quality, longevity, and social responsibility.

Mindful consumption, the focus of Chapter 3, encourages us to re-evaluate our relationship with clothing and embrace a more intentional approach to building our wardrobes. By curating a conscious closet filled with versatile and timeless pieces, we can reduce our environmental impact, support ethical brands, and cultivate a deeper appreciation for the clothes we wear.

The fabric of the future, as explored in Chapter 4, lies in the development and adoption of sustainable materials. From organic cotton and hemp to recycled fibers and innovative bio-based materials, these fabrics offer a more eco-friendly alternative to conventional textiles, reducing pollution, conserving resources, and promoting a circular economy.

The slow fashion movement, discussed in Chapter 5, champions a return to quality, craftsmanship, and timeless design. By embracing slow fashion, we can reject the disposable culture of fast fashion and invest in garments that are made to last, thereby reducing waste and supporting ethical production practices.

Circular fashion, the focus of Chapter 6, envisions a closed-loop system for the fashion industry, where garments are designed to be reused, repaired, or recycled at the end of their life. This approach aims to minimize waste, conserve resources, and create a more sustainable and equitable fashion system.

Fair trade fashion, highlighted in Chapter 7, ensures that the people who make our clothes are treated fairly and paid a living wage. By supporting fair trade brands, we can contribute to the empowerment of workers and the economic development of communities around the world.

Secondhand chic, celebrated in Chapter 8, offers a sustainable and affordable way to express our personal style. By embracing thrifting and vintage shopping, we can reduce waste, discover unique treasures, and contribute to a circular economy.

DIY and upcycling, explored in Chapter 9, empower us to take ownership of our clothes and transform them into unique and personalized pieces. By learning new skills and techniques, we can reduce waste, save money, and express our creativity.

Capsule wardrobes, discussed in Chapter 10, offer a minimalist approach to fashion that prioritizes versatility and functionality. By curating a small collection of essential pieces, we can simplify our lives, reduce decision fatigue, and embrace a more sustainable lifestyle.

Discovering ethical brands, the focus of Chapter 11, allows us to support businesses that align with our values and contribute to a more sustainable and equitable fashion industry. By choosing brands that prioritize transparency, fair labor practices, and eco-friendly materials, we can make a positive impact with our purchasing decisions.

Greenwashing, the subject of Chapter 12, is a deceptive marketing practice that undermines genuine efforts towards sustainability. By learning to identify and reject greenwashing, we can hold brands accountable and ensure that our purchases support truly sustainable practices.

Fashion activism, explored in Chapter 13, harnesses the power of fashion to drive social and environmental change. By using our voices and creativity, we can raise awareness, challenge the status quo, and advocate for a more just and sustainable fashion industry.

Sustainable style icons, celebrated in Chapter 14, inspire us to embrace ethical fashion and make conscious choices about our clothing consumption. By showcasing sustainable brands and promoting conscious consumerism, these icons are paving the way for a more ethical and responsible fashion future.

Wardrobe care, the focus of Chapter 15, is an essential aspect of sustainable fashion. By adopting simple practices, such as proper washing, drying, and storing, we can extend the lifespan of our clothes, reduce waste, and minimize our environmental impact.

Minimalist fashion, discussed in Chapter 16, embraces simplicity, functionality, and timeless elegance. By prioritizing quality over quantity and focusing on essential pieces, we can simplify our lives, reduce consumption, and create a more sustainable wardrobe.

Sustainable accessories, explored in Chapter 17, offer ethical choices for shoes and bags. By choosing brands that prioritize fair labor practices, eco-friendly materials, and sustainable production methods, we can reduce our environmental footprint and support a more ethical fashion industry.

ᗡᗡᗡ

Citation And References

This book represents the culmination of extensive research and meticulous analysis, incorporating a diverse range of sources, including numerous books, scholarly studies, and personal experiences. Additionally, I have scoured various websites to gather relevant information and data essential for the compilation of this work. I have taken every precaution to ensure the accuracy of the information presented and have diligently cited all sources to acknowledge their contributions.

Despite these efforts, the possibility of inadvertent errors remains. I deeply value the insights of my readers and appreciate any feedback that can help identify and rectify such inaccuracies. I encourage you to bring any discrepancies to my attention.

Your feedback is not only welcome but crucial, as it will aid in correcting current editions and enhancing the content of future ones. I am committed to maintaining the highest standards of accuracy and reliability in my work and thank you for your support and understanding.

Additionally, I firmly uphold the principle of freedom of speech and expression as guaranteed under Article 19(1)(a) of the Constitution of India, and I respect the diverse viewpoints and expressions of all readers.

ᖰᖰᖰ

Other Books Of The Author

1. Empowering Minds: A Journey into Women's Self-Discovery and Power
2. The Dynamics of Motivation: Catalyzing Thought into Action
3. Meditation and Mental Well Being: The Path to Inner Peace and Clarity
4. The Psychology of Child Education: Nurturing Future Generations
5. Ethical Enlightenment: A Modern Guide to Living with Integrity
6. Voices of Empowerment: Stories of Women Rising Against Odds
7. Social Psychology in Everyday Life: Understanding Human Connections
8. The Essence of Motivational Speaking: Inspiring Change in Others
9. Balancing Acts: Women, Work, and the Will to Lead
10. Guiding with Grace: Raising Children with Compassion and Awareness
11. The Power of Positive Aging: Embracing Life After Fifty
12. Building Resilient Communities: Social Work in Action
13. The Ethical Educator: Principles for Teaching and Learning
14. From Insight to Impact: Social Psychology for a Better World
15. The Ethics of Empathy: A Guide to Ethical Living
16. The Science of Empowering the Self: Navigating Life's Challenges with Psychological Wisdom
17. The Mindful Conscious Leader: Meditation Techniques for Modern Management
18. Pioneering Spirit: Women's Pathways to Leadership and Empowerment
19. Feeling to Healing: The Role of Emotional Intelligence in Child Development
20. Transformative Talks and Words of Inspiration: Insights into Motivational Oratory

Bhajan
101. Pilgrimage of the Soul: Spiritual Journeys in India

❧❧❧

Contact

Dr. Minakshi Bansal
Social Activist
Ahmedabad, Gujarat, Bharat
minakshiindiag20@yahoo.com

ᑅᑅᑅ

|| LOKAHA SAMASTHAHA SUKHINO BHAVANTU ||